BUTOH
Shades of Darkness

BUTOH

Shades of Darkness

Jean Viala   Nourit Masson-Sekine

Text: Jean Viala
Book Design: Toshiaki Suzuki

Editor: Nourit Masson-Sekine

All rights reserved. No part of this book
may be reproduced in any form without permission
in writing from the publisher.

© Copyright 1988 in Japan
by Jean Viala and Nourit Masson-Sekine

First printing, 1988
Second printing, 1991

Published by Shufunotomo Co., Ltd.
2-9, Kanda Surugadai, Chiyoda-ku, Tokyo, 101 Japan

Printed in Japan

ISBN4-07-974630-X

NOTE
For the transcription of Japanese words into English we have used the Hepburn system of romanization, the system in widest use today. Japanese vowels are pronounced **a** as in f*a*ther, **e** as in r*e*d, **i** as in mar*i*ne, **o** as in s*o*lo, and **u** as in r*u*le. Long vowels are topped with a macron, as in *buyō*.

We have made one major exception in romanization, the word *butoh*, in order to be consistent with the roman spelling commonly used by butoh performers themselves. Certain performance titles have not been translated into English at the request of the artist concerned. We hope that readers will not find this inconsistency too disturbing.

Acknowledgements

This book would not have been possible without the help of Akiko Motofuji and the members of Asbestos Theater, Nario Gōda and Mitsutoshi Hanaga, who graciously provided us with information as well as with various documents. We would like to thank Jacob Raz for writing the foreword, Bela Grushka and Matthew Jocelyn for translating the original French text, Johnny Barrett for translating the Japanese texts, Anne Pepper and Deborah Golden for the proofreading. We also thank all the butoh dancers who were kind enough to collaborate with us. Thanks to Jean-Marie Allaux and Yori Sekine for their encouragement and advice as well as to Odile Salomon.

Special thanks must go to Mrs. Kazuo Ōno, Mr. Yoshito Ōno and the entire Ōno family for their warm welcome during our stay in Japan.

Finally, we would like to express our deepest gratitude and immense admiration for Kazuo Ōno, to whom this book is dedicated.

CONTENTS

Acknowledgements — 5

Watching Butoh — 8

Foreword: Turbulent Years — 10

Introduction: The Birth of Butoh — 16

Chapter I **Kazuo Ōno:** The Soul of Butoh — 20

His Life — 23

Admiring La Argentina — 28

Ozen — 38

My Mother — 41

Dead Sea — 45

A Class with Kazuo Ōno — 55

Chapter II **Tatsumi Hijikata:** The Architect of Butoh — 60

Beginnings — 62

Hijikata and Ashikawa — 84

Hakutōbō — 88

The Return of Hijikata — 92

Chapter III **Hijikata's Legacy** — 98

Dairakuda-kan — 100

Sankai-juku — 108

Byakko-sha — 116

Dance Love Machine — 122

Sebi and Ariadone — 127

Muteki-sha — 132

Hoppō Butoh-ha and Suzurantō — 138

Two People for Three Nights — 139

Chapter IV Improvisational Butoh ———•146

Akira Kasai ———•147

Mitsutaka Ishii ———•152

Min Tanaka ———•158

Teru Goi ———•164

The New Generation of Butoh ———•165

On the Fringes of Butoh ———•170

Chapter V Evolutionary Changes ———•171

Appendix Notes on Butoh

Notes by Kazuo Ōno ———•176

Notes by Tatsumi Hijikata ———•184

Notes by Natsuyuki Nakanishi ———•190

Notes by Eikō Hosoe ———•191

Notes by Kazuko Shiraishi ———•192

Notes by Isamu Ōsuka (Byakko-sha) ———•195

Notes by Ushio Amagatsu (Sankai-juku) ———•196

Notes by Akaji Maro (Dairakuda-kan) ———•197

Notes by Anzu Furukawa ———•198

Notes by Yōko Ashikawa ———•199

Notes by Ebisu Tōri & Min Tanaka ———•200

Notes by Mitsutaka Ishii & Natsu Nakajima ———•201

Photographers ———•202

Photo Credits ———•202

List of Names ———•205

Glossary ———•206

Watching Butoh

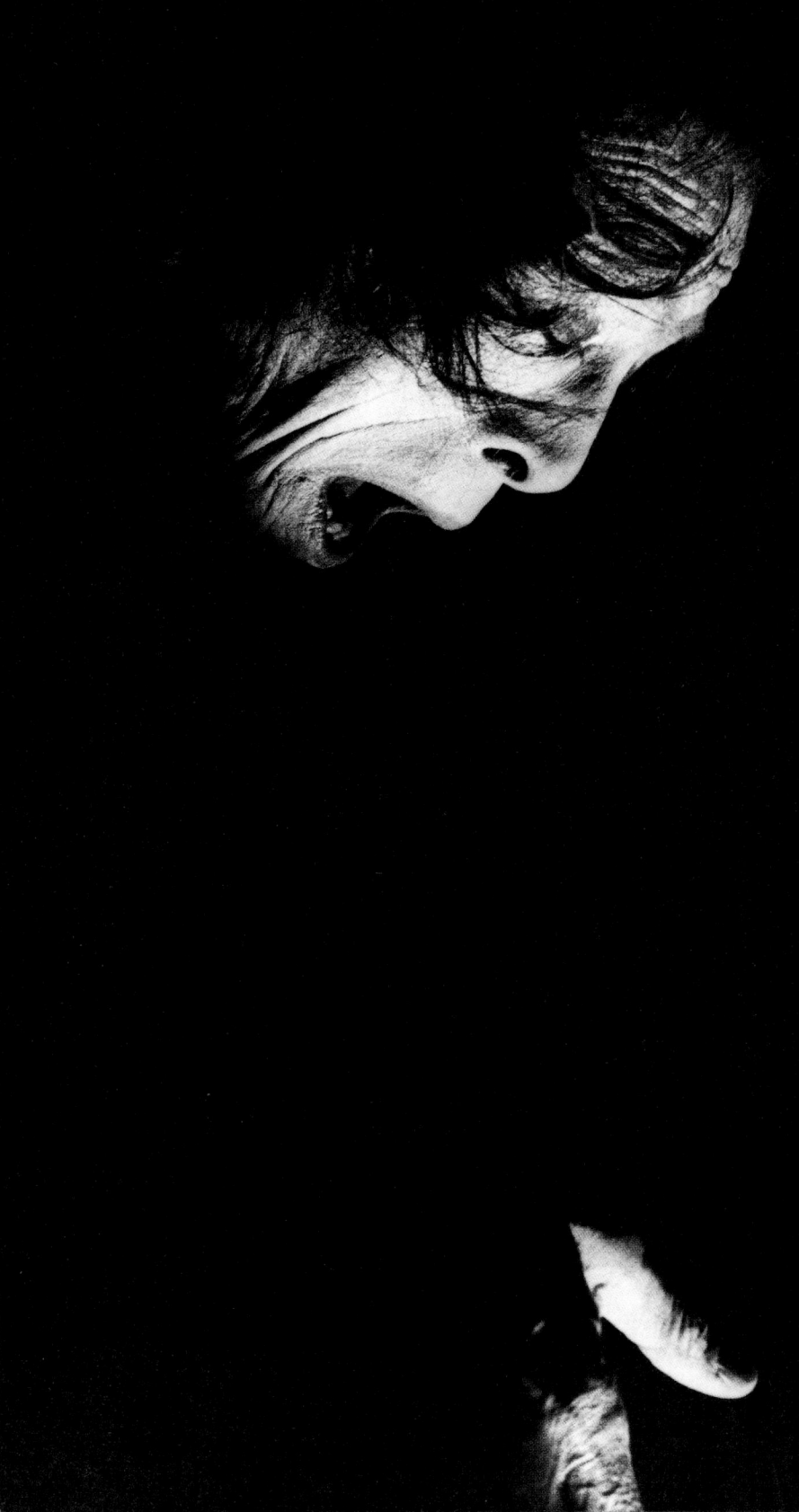

Watching the dance, the eye constantly on the alert, the finger click-ready, gauging the chasms and hues of the darkness, manipulating the presence of the dancer's body in space, ever attentive to the least sign of life.

The silent mise-en-scene unfolds like a love story shrouded in stillness, a dimension of wavering visions and fluctuating meanings. The spontaneous and reciprocal interaction unveils itself on the spur of the moment.

Photographing butoh involves perceiving the unperceived, feeling the emotional chasms locked within a body, watching for the many subtle nuances in expression and the violent contrasts of light and shadow. Paradoxically, the lighting is not always used to pinpoint the dance but to illuminate the depth and shades of darkness out of which the life emerges.

The photographer is witness to a spiritual experience, albeit a sacrilegious witness since he, in attempting to eternalize the experience, falsifies it. The dance exists for no more than a single moment and then disappears into the vacuum of time; the photographer's quixotic pursuit in seeking to capture this fleeting moment leads only to a simulation of the experience.

The extreme concentration and determination of the photographer is evident during the performance or the practice session, film-rolls winding, the hasty click-click of the shutter interspersed by nervous silences and the unfolding play of shadow and light, pose and movement, anxiously awaiting the quintessential moment.

The interaction often takes the form of

a chase, at times frontal, at times circular; the photographer becomes the hunter chasing a prey that lies outside his field of vision; he himself becomes part of the dance by hunting illusions, combating the flux of time and seeking to halt its flow towards death.

The frozen image of the dance is a portrayal of the constant conflict between the opposing natures within the photographer himself: the longing for eternal life and ineluctable death. The image is but a portrayal of one of these fleeting moments.

This book attempts to present a photographic record of the visual experience of butoh. The photographs were taken in many different locations and settings; some posters and pamphlets are also included. These images are an integral part of the butoh world, close in spirit and often possessing the same textural qualities as the dance itself.

I owe deep gratitude to Natsu Nakajima and Ishii Mitsutaka, my two close friends, who introduced me to Mr. Ōno and helped me to understand the world of butoh.

We would particularly like to thank Mr. Mitsutoshi Hanaga, photo-journalist and faithful follower of butoh, who kindly gave us permission to use his negatives to retrace the footsteps of butoh through the 60s and 70s. Our heartfelt gratitude is also due to Mr. Eikō Hosoe, who has generously contributed to this book and has allowed us to use some of his previously unpublished photographs. Our thanks are also extended to all the photographers who have contributed to this book.

Nourit Masson-Sekine

Foreword
Turbulent Years

Hippies in the streets of Tokyo in the late 60's.

Street event in the late 60's.

Demonstration in front of the Diet Building.

Nineteen sixty was one of the most turbulent years in postwar Japan. It was in that year that the Japanese government, supported by the conservatives and violently opposed by the left, approved the renewal of the U.S.-Japan Mutual Security Treaty which permitted U.S. military bases on Japanese soil. For months the nation was torn by debate and demonstrations over the question of the treaty. The demonstrations culminated on June 15, 1960, when the demonstrators forced their way into the Diet compound and one of their members, Michiko Kamba, lost her life in the confused struggle that followed.

Butoh, with its roots predating the turbulent 1960s, has never been a politically oriented movement. Nevertheless, the movement began to take shape around 1960, and one cannot fully understand it without some knowledge of the political, social and artistic context of the time.

Nineteen sixty was a turning point. It marked the end of the road of the 1945 defeat, the first in Japan's history, and of the years of American occupation, which had brought dramatic changes in political and social values, among them imposed democracy, a new constitution, new civil law, and fast urbanization.

The relationship of the United States to Japan was in itself a confusing and challenging issue in 1960. The hitherto enemy was now best friend. The conservatives (the former "nationalists") who had cooperated with the occupation now supported the renewal of the treaty. The leftists (the former "traitors") now sought an independent, more "nationalist" policy.

Many Japanese felt inferior when confronted with American culture, which gave rise to a fervent desire to attain equal standing with America in both economic and cultural affairs. But there was an ambivalence among the people in taking America for their model. After all, the United States was their recent enemy. But modernization meant Americanization, and this created conflicting feelings.

The ensuing changes in the institution of the family and the agricultural land reform transformed the traditional patterns of human relations. The old family structure fell apart, and the new civil law defined new relationships between men and women, husbands and wives. Rapid urbanization brought about the emergence of the huge *danchi*, or condominiums, which put an end to the old intimate relationships of the neighborhood and the village.

Thus, the Japanese were torn between an obsession with "progress" and refuge in nostalgia. A new folklore boom emerged, centered on the works of folklorist Kunio Yanagita. This boom offered an opportunity to escape from modernism, and to dig into the deeper layers of Japanese tradition and values. Needless to say, this did not stop modernization, nor did it attempt to do so. The sense of tragedy portrayed in literary and performing art works of the time comes from the feeling of profound confusion that could neither be overcome nor resolved. Modernization could not be accepted, but neither could it be fought. It could only be laughed at, escaped from via nostalgia and "tradition," or dug into and reconstructed, as a nightmare image on stage.

On the literary scene, a reappraisal of the values of prewar Japanese literature could be seen in both literary works and criticism. Since the 1880s, Japanese literature had been oscillating between rejection and defense of traditional writing. But in the 1950s, the typically Japanese "I-novel" (*shi-shōsetsu*) with its personal, introverted style—hitherto considered outmoded—found new popularity because it was seen to represent opposition to the pressures of the modern urban age.

Writers such as Junichiro Tanizaki, Yasunari Kawabata, Ōsamu Dazai and Yukio Mishima resisted certain Western influences in their works. Some deliberately adopted traditional values, thus opposing the tendency of Western literature to present moral, political or philosophical judgements, or to serve as a vehicle for exploring or declaring new truths—all of which are contrary to the spirit of Japanese literature. In the days of defeat and despair, lyricism and gentle melancholy, or a sense of the ephemeral quality of life were features that best expressed the period's mood of confusion, sorrow and insecurity. Sometimes seeded with existentialist or Marxist ideas, this mood took nihilistic, absurd, or lyrical forms. The strong feeling for design and convention, the use of word-play, the

Art performance by the Group Zero, 1968.

fragmentary style—all these were no longer rejected as weaknesses.

A new experimental mood flourished in Japan. In 1950, the Jikken Kōbō (Experimental Studio) was formed by a group of artists from dance, literature, music, photography and fine arts. Participants included composers, such as Tōru Takemitsu and Shin-ichi Suzuki, artists, such as Yamaguchi, music critics, such as Akiyama, and performers, such as Sonoda and Nagamatsu. Among other innovations, these artists revolutionized the old notions of the strict teacher-student relationship. Simultaneously, many other experimental groups emerged, such as the Directors' Colloquium, Hachi no Kai (a group of poets and composers), Neo-Dadaism Organizers, Japan Underground Center, and others.

On the music scene, composer Matsudaira received an international award in 1952 for his composition "Theme and Variations for Piano and Orchestra" in which he linked the twelve-tone technique with *gagaku*, one of the oldest Japanese musical genres. In the following years, composers wrote in various styles such as musique concrete and electronic music. By the late 1950s, Japanese composers felt they had already caught up with the innovations of European music. Japanese music was influenced by both Western ideas and a rediscovery of the possibilities of Japanese traditional music.

The early 1960s were marked by the influence of John Cage (who visited Japan), and the works of his followers. His idea of metaphysical aesthetics, his use of musical chance and his desire to create music free of taboo affected the Japanese scene. Performers began to collaborate with composers from the early stages of the creation of the work, and "group music" groups were formed, based on improvisation. Players of traditional instruments—*shakuhachi, shamisen, biwa, koto*—began to show interest in performing modern music with traditional instruments. The "irrational"character of traditional music, considered outmoded and incompatible with Western music, was now valued as a unique feature to be used as an independent element in modern music. An example was Tōru Takemitsu's "November Steps," written for *shakuhachi, biwa* and orchestra, in which he emphasized the individual characteristics of both the Western and Japanese instruments.

By the 60s on the theatrical scene, *shingeki*, the theater

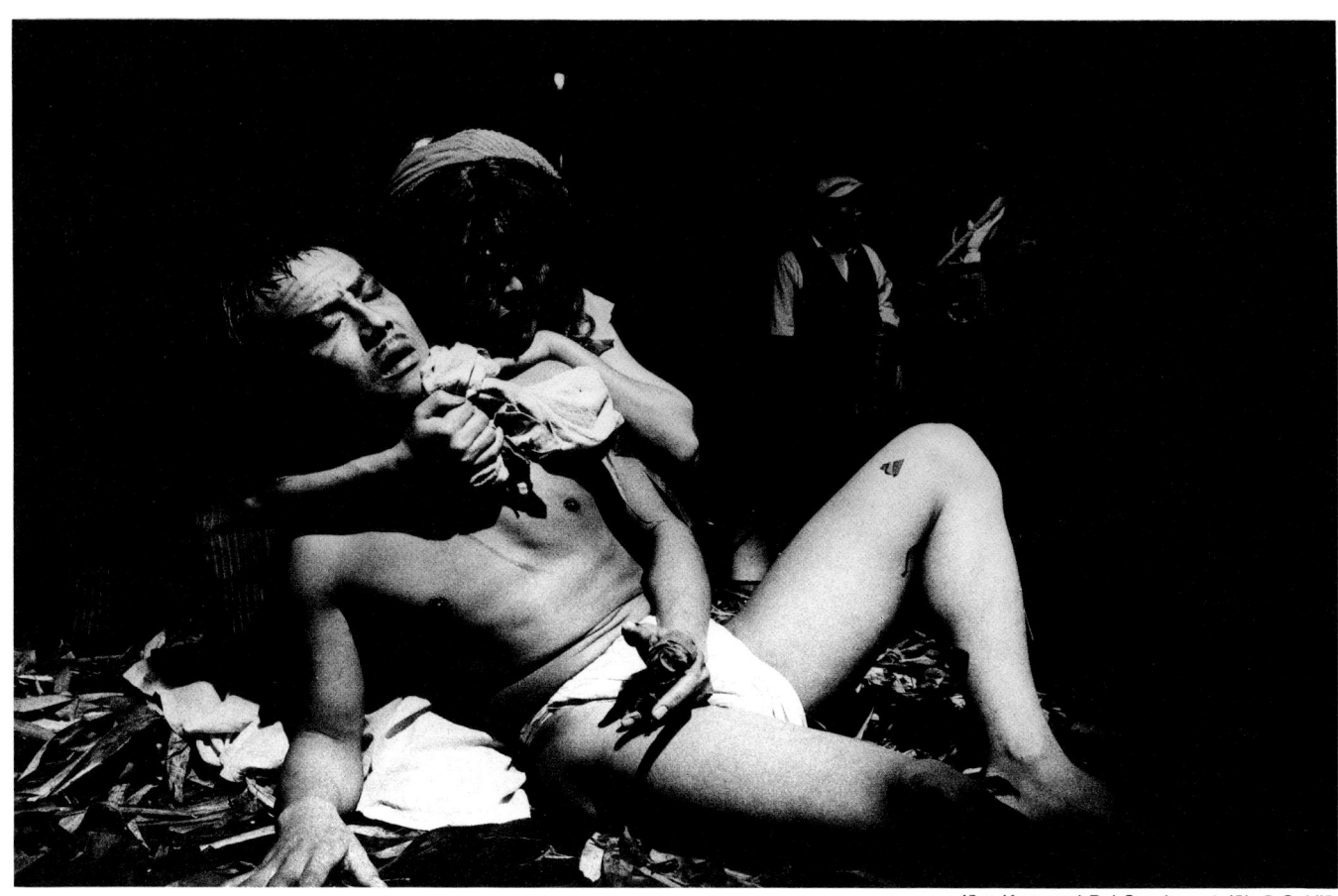

Jūro Kara and Rei Sen Lee at Jōkyō Gekijō.

movement established in the 1920s with the aim of achieving a European style theater, although economically stable and fully recognized, no longer satisfied the younger generation. The young no longer accepted *shingeki*'s commitment to Western realism, themes and aspirations. Numerous alternative groups appeared, most of them emerging from the student theater activity around the events of 1960. Of these, the most influential were the Jōkyō Gekijō (The Theater of Situations), led by Jūro Kara, the Waseda Shōgekijō (Waseda Little Theater) led by Tadashi Suzuki, the Kuro Tento (The Black Tent), led by Shin Satō; and the Tenjō Sajiki (The Gallery), led by Shuji Terayama.

In 1959, the Seinen Geijutsu Gekijō (Seigei)—Youth Art Theater—was established after differences with the older generation over the issue of the Security Treaty, and a feeling that the old theater was no longer relevant to contemporary concerns. It was an expression of political dissent. Seigei was a politically engaged, activist theater, inspired by the political theater of Brecht. Its famous agit-prop play "Document No. 1" dramatized the actual experience of the group's members during the 1960 demonstration. Most of the avant-garde groups mentioned above were

Butoh training directed by T. Hijikata at Asbesto-kan.

in one way or another personally connected with Seigei at the beginning of their creative development.

Jurō Kara's existentialist theater (strongly influenced by Sartre, from whom it took its name) put great emphasis on the use of the environment, and several of his productions symbolized for the entire next generation the rejection of

"The Place is not just a geographical occasion. It is also a historically rooted structure dependent upon specific, ingenious traditions." S. Terayama

Shūji Terayama in the 60's.

theater buildings. He began to perform in a red tent, an example followed by other groups. Setting one of its productions against Shinjuku train station, the busiest in Japan, the Red Tent became the symbol of resistance to the trends of urbanization and modernization epitomized by Shinjuku. Kara's theater was physical, violent, vivid, colorful and predominantly political. He was also the first to make trips to third world countries (Korea, Middle East, Brazil), thus preceding the tours of other avant-garde groups in the 1960s and 1970s.

Tadashi Suzuki and the Waseda Shogekijō were more interested in existential than in political and social concerns. Later, Suzuki came to be interested in traditional acting techniques, and developed the now internationally acclaimed "Suzuki Method."

From Waseda and Tōkyō Universities' Theater study societies, whose members actively participated in the 1960 demonstrations, emerged the June Theater (Rokugatsu Gekijō), in commemoration of the June, 1960, demonstrations. This later developed, under the leadership of Makoto Satō, into the Theater Center 68/69, or the Black Tent.

The avant-garde rejected Western tragedy as a theatrical and philosophical concept together with the idea of the "free individual" so dominant in this tradition. Additionally they rejected the obsession of *shingeki* dramatists with the West and the acceptance of the West as the mainstream of history, with Japan as a marginal, particular case. They insisted on the legitimacy of being different, particular, Japanese, or of being an anomaly. Their aim was to achieve "an anomalous structure that made radical use of universal terms for the express purpose of destroying the universal language."

Both butoh and theater artists in the early 1960s were influenced by the aesthetic of graphic artist Tadanori Yokoo, who designed several sets for them. Yokoo's style was purposely in "bad taste," emphasizing the ugly and the irrational, with the intention of making the unfashionable fashionable. His works frequently made use of daily objects of the late Meiji, Taishō and early Shōwa eras (1910–1930), periods that also inspired many of the butoh and theater artists of the early 1960s. Yokoo, in his sophisticated use of the naive and childish, included cartoon-like drawings, theater bills, old menus, advertisements, posters, and photographs from the beginning of the century. Emphasizing bad taste, the banal, and the embarrassing, Yokoo revolutionized the graphic arts of the early 1960s.

Tadanori Yokoo, Tatsumi Hijikata, Shuji Terayama, Jūro Kara and others created a theater of poverty, a stage that looked like a flea market, using rags and strange combinations of Japanese dresses, or Western and Japanese costumes. There was an intentionally excessive use of cliches and melodrama. Together these created a visual image of a wasteland, as if the stage were the backyard of a dying civilization, filled with spastic gruesome creatures, resembling both real-life Japanese and creatures of fantasy.

Avant-garde artists in dance and theater expressed a strong aversion to art. They attempted to break up all structures into fragile, seemingly meaningless fragments. Often this was done in a merry, childishly happy, party-like atmosphere, as if the artists chose to look at the existential suffering and confusion with laughter.

Plays became extremely complex, using theater-within-theater techniques, multiple plots, and collage-like compositions. In these ways, the avant-garde artists rejected conventional Western-theater concepts in both the theme and structure of the play or the theatrical event. (Needless to say, a similar approach was developing in the West at the same time.)

On the whole, although manifestos and articles written by these artists often rejected Japanese traditions, along with Western influences, most works of both dance and theater of the era were characterized by their strong Japanese flavor, either directly or indirectly. On the stage, one could see, time and again, the kimonos, village baskets, old Shintō costumes, ritual objects and traditional musical instruments. Playwrights from Minoru Betsuyaku to Jūro Kara and Shin Satō made increasing use of Japanese traditional myths, epics and rituals, although in a new and provocative context.

The provocative use of "bad taste," the ugly, the grotesque, and the inversion of aesthetic and social values, on the surface so un-Japanese, is deeply rooted in certain traditions in Japan still surviving in various regions. What is named by several critics (i.e., Masakatsu Gunji) *shūaku no bi* (aesthetics of ugliness) is a legitimate feature of both folk tradition and classical art. Numerous examples of what could be called "rituals of inversion" can be drawn from folk rituals: the grotesque dance of the twisted-faced Hyottoko; the *modoki*, whose function was to ridicule sacred rituals; the *namahage* festival in the north, where youngmen, wearing gruesome masks enter houses with their boots on, shouting and roaring, threatening and frightening children or pinching the bottoms of brides; and the *akutai matsuri*, where participants use abusive language and gestures against fellow participants and priests. In this

Fertility Festival

sense, avant-garde artists of the 1960s were faithful followers of old Japanese traditions, although they put these traditions into new perspectives and proportions.

It might be appropriate to end with Jūro Kara's memories of the war, and thus illustrate the background of the origin of images created by the 1960s avant-garde:

"On the burnt-over plain (left at the end of the war by air raids over Tokyo) of Ueno-Shimo-Kurumazaka, there were the singed remains of a public bath. To a kid like me, who could only imagine what the air-raid had been like by putting the old faucet that had been left there to my ear and listening, there were no grouchy old men and women, secret police or neighborhood associations to send you off to war. As far as my eyes could see, there was not so much as a single person to harm me. But by listening to the voice of that faucet lying on the ground, it was no longer difficult to know the meaning of devastation. That's why I say people of my generation weren't raised by people's stern and reproving glances. We were surrounded and educated by faucets lying on the ground. My mind is too filled with things, like descriptions of characters in Balzac's novels."

Jacob Raz

Naked Festival

Introduction

During the last ten years, at a time when Japan has come to the forefront of the world economy, butoh has managed to attract and win a Western audience. There is not a festival where it does not reign alongside the great names in contemporary dance; butoh now has its place in the cultural communities of New York, Paris and Berlin.

Its discovery has been a shock for many Westerners—and in no way comparable to what Western dance revolutionaries (such as Merce Cunningham or Pina Bausch) are offering. There was no frame of reference: how could we perceive a form of movement, an art, born of a Japanese culture hitherto essentially familiar to us through a series of clichés, especially those pertaining to Japanese dance?

Although audiences have begun to appreciate this new form of dance, certain preconceptions and misunderstandings still persist. It has therefore become indispensable to place butoh in its cultural context, to trace its history, and to point out its essential characteristics.

Our hope is that this book will provide questions and answers for the reader who is interested in new paths of research and will better enable him to comprehend the major phenomenon of contemporary dance which butoh has become.

The Birth of Butoh

In order to understand the unique position of butoh in the artistic landscape of Japan we must first examine the situation of the dance world from which it evolved.

Before the war, there were two major types of dance: traditional dance (mainly *kagura*, *buyō*, *bugaku*, and *nō*), and Western dance (classical ballet and modern dance) brought to Japan in the wave of Western influence which began with the Meiji era.

The early development of modern dance provided the background necessary to the birth of butoh. From modern dance came the idea that dance could be a creative interaction between form and content which might convey the spirit of the times, as opposed to an interpretation of the existing forms used in traditional dance, or the expression of a gestural vocabulary as used in classical ballet.

The first important modern dancer in Japan was Baku Ishii. After studying classical ballet with the Imperial Theater Company in Tōkyō, he studied the Dalcroze Technique and *Neue Danz* with his friend Kōsaku Yamada (who had recently returned from Germany) and eventually dedicated himself to what he called "Creation Dance," part of his "Dance-Poetry" movement. He tried to create new forms, to reveal new concepts, which would allow him to freely express the spirit of his times.

The time was ripe for experimentation. Other young dancers such as Kazuo Ōno and Tatsumi Hijikata had begun to study modern dance and were stimulated by this idea of "creation."

The first butoh dancers attempted to develop Ishii's theories and to find a way to experience and explore modern style without disavowing their Japanese cultural heritage. They had to create a dance which would draw its

Baku Ishii

Ōno and Hijikata in rehearsal.

strength from their country's culture and be representative of the contradictions and impulses of the times.

The movement began in a spirit of revolt. Although these young dancers—Kazuo Ōno, Tatsumi Hijikata, Yoshito Ōno, Mitsutaka Ishii and others—rejected the genre of modern dance, they joined forces to create performances in which they strove to break the rules, to upset existing forms and to shatter the traditional framework of dance. More than performances, these were events or happenings. The dancers were not interested in carefully constructed work. They were concerned with surviving as artists, expressing themselves at all costs. They thought of dance as an intense way of existing, rather than as a vehicle for a message or simply the organization of space.

They did not want to speak through the body, but instead to let the body speak for itself, to disclose truth, to reveal itself in all its authenticity and depth, rejecting the superficiality of everyday life.

A great deal of emphasis was placed on transformations (see page 113), the only way to sublimate the body whose meaning seemed lost in the banality of ordinary existence. The basis of Ōno's work, for instance, was transubstantiation into a "dead body," that of Hijikata, the will to systematically shatter the habits which limit the way we move our bodies and the way we perceive our bodies.

The butoh dancer endeavors to reveal his relationship to his inner world, to the unconscious. Butoh attempts to present the erotic as well as the ascetic dimension of the body by revealing, for example, the element of darkness and perversity which we all carry within. It uses the image of androgeny, whose mixing of sexes and roles epitomizes social disorder.

Above all butoh implies total presence. In order to achieve this the dancer must develop the ability to tune into his body's inner senses, to be sensitive to fluctuations of energy, to explore his relationship to the space around him and to the world. Dancing means "being" in the cosmos, as well as containing the cosmos within oneself. Rather than aspiring to an aesthetic ideal, the dancer attempts to bare his soul, to reveal the human being in his banality, ugliness and grotesqueness, to expose the suffering and joys of life.

Mitsutaka Ishii with K. Ōno and T. Hijikata in "Butoh Genet," 1967.

Tomiko Takai in "Emotion in Metaphysics."

Yoshito Ōno in "Rose-colored Dance."

CHAPTER I

KAZUO ŌNO
THE SOUL OF BUTOH

(Biography written with the help of Mr. Kenshi Ashida and Toshio Mizohata)

1906 Born in Hakodate, Hokkaido.
1926 Entered the Japan Athletic School.
He was very moved when he saw his own body in a big mirror at Matsuya Department Store in Ginza.
1929 Impressed by the performance of a Spanish dancer, La Argentina, he decided to become a dancer. About 50 years later he expressed his gratitude to her in the solo performance "Admiring La Argentina." Graduated from the Athletic School, and started working as a gymnastics teacher.
1933 Started studying at Baku Ishii's Dance School.
1934 Deeply moved by seeing Harald Kreutzberg Dance in Tokyo.
1936 Started studying with Takaya Eguchi.
1938–1946 Served in the army.
1949 Dance performance by Kazuo Ōno and Mitsuko Ando: "Ennui for the City," "Shoes," "A Hat," "Kind God." Kazuo Ōno Modern Dance Concert No. 1: "Devil Cry," "Tango," "First Flower of a Linden Tree."
1950 Kazuo Ōno MDC No. 2: "Festival," "Beyond the Field," "Harp of Zion," "Spring Offering," "Lotus Wandering Child," etc.
1951 Kazuo Ōno MDC No. 3: "Spring Tide," "Downtown Dance."
1952 Enchanted by "Les Enfants du Paradis" by Marcel Carné.
1953 Kazuo Ōno Group MDC: "Stray Thoughts," "Fox and a Stone Figure," "Fruits in the Heaven."
1954 Guest appearance for "Mitsuko Ando Dance Heels." Gets to know Tatsumi Hijikata.
1959 Kazuo Ōno Dance Concert: "The Old Man and the Sea."
1960 "Notre Dame des Fleurs" (From Genêt) and "Treatment Spot" (from Maldoror's Songs); choreographed by T. Hijikata.
1961 "Secret Ceremony for an Hermaphrodite," "Sugar Cake," etc.; choreographed by T. Hijikata.
1965 "Rose-Colored Dance"; choreographed by T. Hijikata.
1966 "Illustrated Book of Sexology Instruction—Tomato," directed by T. Hijikata.
1968 Guest performance in M. Ishii's "O Genêt."
1969 Movie "A Portrait of Mr. O," directed by Chiaki Nagano.
1971 Movie "Mandala of Mr. O," directed by C. Nagano.
1973 Movie "The Book of a Dead Man, Mr. O," directed by C. Nagano.
1977 "Celebrating La Argentina," solo; choreographed by T. Hijikata.
1980 "Ozen," K. Ōno Co.; choreographed by K. Ōno.
1981 "My Mother," solo; choreographed by T. Hijikata.
1985 "Dead Sea," duo with Yoshito Ōno.
1987 Monet's "Waterlillies," duo with Yoshito Ōno.
1988 "Insect Metamorphosis" with Yoshito Ōno.
1990 Published his book, "The Palace Soars into the Sky." "Kachō Fūgetsu" with Yoshito Ōno.

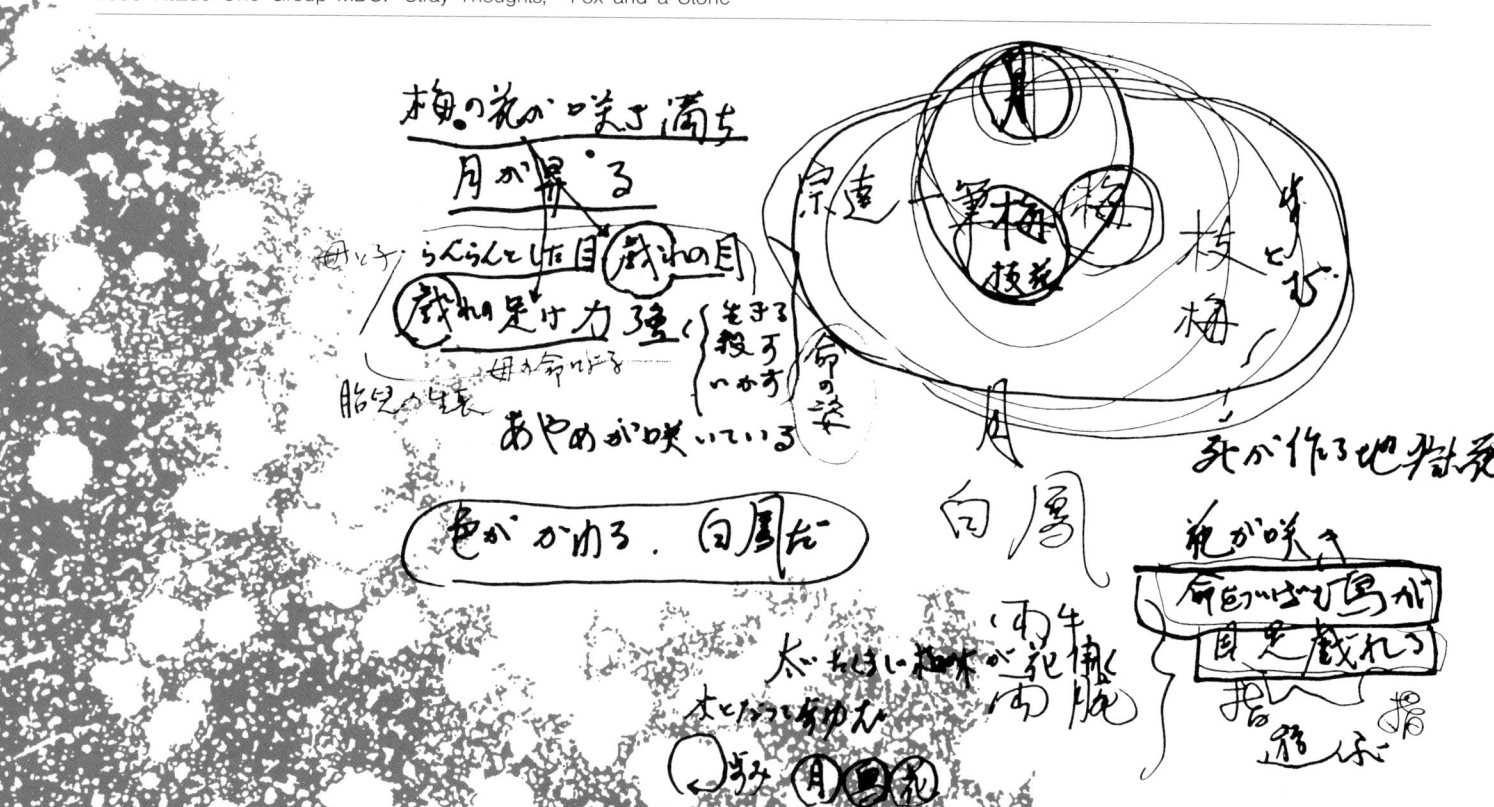

A lesson of modern dance.

"Il pleure dans mon cœur comme il pleut sur la ville." Verlaine

Like a window open to the light, Kazuo Ōno stands at the heart of butoh. Tirelessly seeking to renew himself, he is still, at his eighties, enlivening butoh with fresh ideas.

Ōno's strength resides in his exceptional coherence and unity: man and artist are one. His private existence and his work as an artist both meet the same exacting demands. This is why his very presence is in itself an artistic fact, an event.

Ōno believes. He believes in God, and to him his faith is as essential as breathing; it can be found in the depths of his being and in his daily gestures. He believes in human beings and in their potential for love and generosity. He believes in life, that force which inhabits the universe, from the tiniest grain of sand to the stars themselves. And he dances to communicate the joy of being a man, alive on this earth.

Dance, says Ōno, should be capable of representing the universal in its purest and most abstract expression. As the branches of a tree grow toward the sky only if its roots are anchored in the earth, so dance must penetrate the depths of daily existence. If it remains too close to daily life, it reminds us of mime and cannot throw light on the confusion of reality. If too abstract, all connection with reality disappears and the audience fails to be moved.

Ōno believes that dance should reveal the "form of the soul," and to achieve this the dancer must separate himself from his physical and social identity.

Ōno says that butoh revolves around the idea of the "dead body," into which the dancer places an emotion which can then freely express itself. Without this technique, the "living body" would divert the emotion, drawing it into its own logic. He tells us that as the puppeteer pulls the strings, the soul should guide the artist.

He often speaks of the "freedom" of the dancer. This must be understood in the eastern sense: it does not mean "free will," but rather shaking off the confines of free will, liberation from narrow thoughts and individuality. Dancing freely means giving up the notion of oneself, reverting to the original memory of the body, and discovering the soul stifled within.

This preoccupation is reminiscent of Jerzy Grotowski, who believed that to attain the universal we must break all rigidity, the fixed patterns which our bodies have acquired over the years. Once our shell is cracked, truth will express itself in all its strength.

Ōno's work on the "dead body" makes the same demands. As long as the body maintains an existence marked by social experience, it cannot express the soul with purity.

In order to make himself clear, Ōno often makes this analogy: "If you wish to dance a flower, you can mime it and it will be everyone's flower, banal and uninteresting; but if you place the beauty of that flower and the emotions which are evoked by it into your dead body, then the flower you create will be true and unique and the audience will be moved."

The issues of life and death lie at the heart of his work. His dance, which he states is a "creation of the world," is a mystique, a revelation of being, the meeting of man with life. Therein lies its force and grandeur.

His Life

Hokkaido, where Ōno was born, is Japan's equivalent of the American Frontier, a wide open, spacious land settled in the 19th century by adventurous people with a pioneer spirit.

Born in 1906, he spent his childhood in Hokkaido. After graduating from university in 1925, he became a school teacher. Dissatisfied, he left after a year and went to Tōkyō where he enrolled in the National School of Athletics.

That year, Ōno was very disturbed to see the reflection of his body in the mirror of a Ginza department store. He was to recall this vision at various times during his life and he still believes that this initial questioning of his image was what led him to seek his identity in dance. Could there be a more beautiful answer than dance to the anxiety caused by the meaning of his body?

In 1929, his friend Yoshio Monden took him to see the Spanish dancer, La Argentina, at the Imperial Theater. The deep emotion which he experienced that day was never to leave him, and fifty years

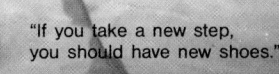
"If you take a new step, you should have new shoes."

Y. Ōno and K. Ōno in "The Room."

later he created "Admiring La Argentina," his most famous performance.

After graduating from the School of Athletics, he worked as a gymnastics teacher in a private school in Yokohama for five years. Later, he embraced the Christian faith and was baptized. Christianity was to remain his major source of inspiration.

Ōno began studying modern dance in 1933 with Baku Ishii. In 1934 he saw a performance in Tokyo by Harald Kreutzberg which had a lasting influence on him. In 1936, he began dance classes with Takaya Eguchi, who had studied *Neue Danz* in Germany with Mary Wigman. He was drafted into the army in 1938 and was unable to study with Eguchi again until 1946.

He performed his first recital, a series of very short pieces, in 1949. He was forty-three years old at the time. Other performances followed in 1950 and 1951.

During this period, he was primarily concerned with methods of expression. He tried to convey moods and feelings, but admits that he wasn't very clear about what it was he was so fervently trying to express.

1954 marked his first meeting with Tatsumi Hijikata, and their collaboration first bore fruit in 1959 with a performance entitled "The Old Man and the Sea," based on an adaptation of the Hemingway novel by Nobuo Ikemiya and choreographed by Hijikata.

For this performance, Ōno became more systematic in his study of expression. "There was the sky above the boat, the boat on the sea, and the fish under the water. Life is everywhere and I wanted to express all of this at once," he says. During rehearsals, he fainted at the end of the dance. "Will I faint on the day of the performance?" he asked himself. And he did. For the first time, another kind of dance revealed itself within him. In his own words, he had "come face to face with my soul." But he did not fully understand this profound art form until 1960 in his next show, "Divine," which marked the turning point of his career. In this adaption of Jean Genêt's novel, choreographed by Hijikata, Ōno played the role of Divine.

"I did not know Genêt's work," explains Ōno, "but Hijikata told me, 'You will be Divine, you will be a transvestite.' And without having read Genêt, without understanding him, I became Divine. I often wonder if I could have done it had I understood . . . but I had a premonition of another world. This performance was my encounter with Genêt, my encounter with Hijikata, my encounter

T. Hijikata and K. Ōno in "Rose-colored Dance," 1965

25

with myself. I cannot explain the word 'encounter,' and I do not want to. My dance is an encounter with Mankind, an encounter with Life. But I cannot forget that we all sleep upon Death, and that our lives are carried by the thousands of dead that came before us and who we will soon join.

"If we decide intellectually what we wish to do, the dance we perform will be dead. A very small thing can make a very great work, a very small experience from life which we carry in our heart and allow to take form."

Ōno continued to work with Hijikata for several shows: "The Songs of Maldoror" (1960), "Secret Ceremony for an Hermaphrodite" (1961), "Sweet Cake" (1961), "Pink Dance" (1965), "Instructions on Sexual Effect" and "Tomato" (1966).

Between 1967 and 1977 he participated in the shows of Tomiko Takai, Mitsutaka Ishii, Akira Kasai, and others. In 1969 he appeared in his first dance film, "Portrait of Mr. O," directed by Chiaki Nagano, followed by "The Mandala of Mr. O" in 1971 and "The Book of a Dead Man: Mr. O" in 1973.

These films are constructed as a sequence of poetic or surrealistic scenes, without a narrative structure. As in Ōno's dance performances, they are presented as a series of images which undergo continuous transformations by means of analogy and juxtaposition. In 1974, he danced in "Forbidden Dish" and in 1975 collaborated with Yasuko Takeuchi in "The Song of Narcissus." But these were only short pieces contained within the works of his friends.

Between 1967 and 1976, he did not perform and appeared to have left the stage. Nevertheless, his strong desire to dance continued to grow.

It was an unexpected incident which finally brought him back to the stage. In 1976 he was invited to the exhibition of his painter friend, Natsuyuki Nakanishi. Standing stupefied before one of the paintings, he exclaimed, "This is La Argentina!"

La Argentina was Antonia Mercé, the Spanish dancer who had so impressed him fifty years earlier. After all this time her recital remained his most vivid theatrical memory. This second encounter with La Argentina was the sign for which he had been waiting in order to resume dancing. A few months later he created "Admiring La Argentina" which was first performed at the Dai-Ichi Seimei Hall in Tokyo.

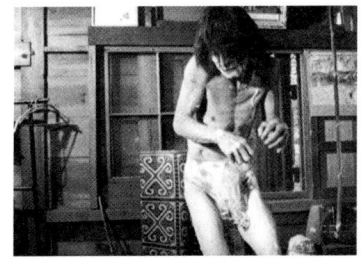

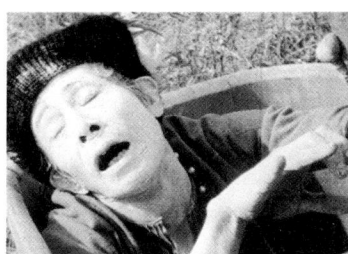

Photo Series from
Chiaki Nagano
Movies
1969~73

Admiring La Argentina

Those fortunate enough to have seen this show remember it with emotion. In it, Ōno conjures up life and death, youth and old age, love and suffering. Rediscovering the cycles and transformations of the ephemeral, he carries us through eternity and offers us man's truth in all its grandeur and derision.

Death and Birth

At the beginning we see only a large feathered hat in the first row of the audience. Slowly, with great difficulty, a ghostly aging theatrical star rises and to a background of Maria Callas singing "Manon Lescaut," clumsily makes her way toward the stage. Heavily made up, covered with lace, she clings desperately to the illusory thread of life, and turns as if to cast a last glance upon her past before staggering onto the stage, quietly ascending towards death. She covers the ground with her cape and gently lies down upon it to die.

Death is followed by birth: the old woman recalls her childhood and is transformed into a young girl—La Argentina—who throws herself joyfully into youth and life.

Everyday Life/The Marriage of Earth and Sky
While the first part is illustrative, the second part, "Daily Life," appears more abstract and spiritual. This is the scene which Ōno holds most dear and which best exemplifies his concept of dance.

Here, the "Marriage of Earth and Sky" (or the creation of the universe) is developed. This marriage of opposites, which is also found in the image of the androgyne or transvestite, constitutes one of the most fundamental tenets of Ōno's work: it makes possible the escape from a surface reality in order to attain the essence of life.

In this scene, there are no more images, but rather the hard reality of everyday life. The gestures are simple and the forms elementary: he walks, kneels, stands with his arms raised toward the sky. Silence. The man is there before our eyes. Real. He wears only a pair of black shorts and we see the traces of life which time has engraved on his body. Metaphor of existence: there is a human being here before us, struggling with the vicissitudes of life, its joys, pains and fears. Anxiety: we feel death arising from somewhere in the silence between the hammering footsteps on the stage.

The second act is a game played with La Argentina. She says, "Come Ōno, dance with me." This expressive solo is almost an "archeology" of Ōno's art, as it bears the marks of his career as a dancer, especially his memories of modern dance (his studies with Takaya Eguchi, his memories of Harald Kreutzberg, and of all the past performances which have left their impression on him).

He is now beyond life and death; only the pleasure of the game, the innocence of the moment remains. Ōno's dance leads us through a veritable battle with space. He smiles. He laughs. It is the moment when dreams come true, when fantasies become reality. We are guests at a great celebration of reconciliation with the universe, an enormous outburst of enthusiasm and love.

In the finale, he reappears accompanied by the voice of Maria Callas, as if she were an avatar of La Argentina and he could play within her. As simple as a child, Ōno wholeheartedly offers himself to his audience, improvising his curtain calls—the last "thank yous"—with the naive pleasure of dancing. During a visit to Paris he was given a rare recording of La Argentina playing the castanets and he added these short pieces to his recital as a final homage to Spain, to dance, and to Antonia Mercé.

"I feel crushed and want to cry, want to play, want to die, want to live."

Ozen

For the Festival of Nancy in 1980 (his first appearance abroad), in addition to "Admiring La Argentina," Ōno choreographed a performance for himself and four other dancers: "Ozen" (The Table).

It is his own story which he tells in this work, centered upon the little table which the Japanese use in the ceremonies which mark the important life events (birth, marriage, entering university). It is a kind of mirror of memories.

The various tableaux which vividly illustrate the life of the fetus, the meal with the mother, birth, and so on, unfold to the music of the *shamisen* and the folk tunes of the northern regions where Ōno spent his childhood. This piece, performed only once, was more concrete than "My Mother," which grew out of it two years later.

"I think everybody has a table that was made for him before he was born."

My Mother

"I don't believe that the body can transform itself, unless it undergoes the fundamental changes of life and death. Therefore, when I try to prove my own existence it is impossible not to follow the thread of my memories until I reach my mother's womb: for it is there that my life began. So I try to carry in my body all the weight and mystery of life; and I believe dance is born of this experience."

In "My Mother," Ōno tried to create a performance about the very source and essence of his dance, stripped of the descriptive images which could be found in "Admiring La Argentina." Ōno sought the heart of butoh. The challenge of "My Mother" was to create a purely spiritual dance. The initial version consisted of three parts, the first of which was itself divided into three tableaux: The Dream of the Fetus, The Dream of the Mother, and The Testament.

The Dream of the Fetus

The stage is bare, bathed in golden light. We hear a vague rumbling, the sort of sound mass that a fetus might hear in its mother's womb. Ōno, his torso draped in white cloth fastened at the back by a string of little knots suggesting an embryonic spine, stands on the stage, an infant in the womb. The flower he holds in his hand is a token of the love he bears for his mother.

He lives. His dance is the incarnation of his emotions. Images go through his mind: childhood memories, the memory of a drawing by William Blake, a game played in a barn, a ship's mast... all these take form in his body.

Drawing the threads of the past towards himself, he encounters his mother.

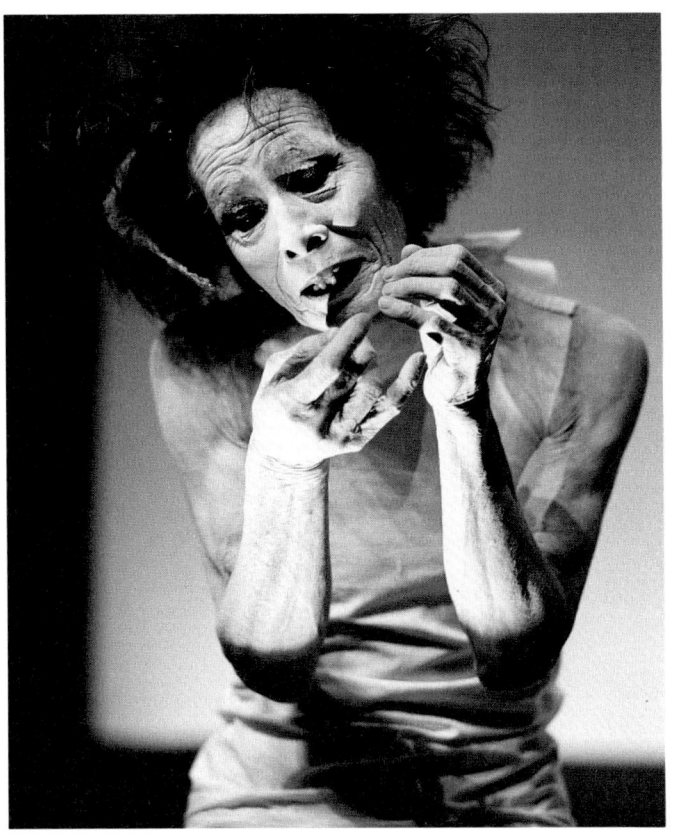

The Dream of the Mother
"The dead also dream."

The rumbling sound has become the crackling music of flames at the stake. He remembers his mother eating, playing the *shamisen*, sewing in a corner. What was she thinking about? What was she dreaming? He recalls the death of his younger sister, crushed by a bus.

In this tableau he dresses himself in an old beige kimono, sticks a flower in his hair, and becomes the Mother. She dreams. She dreams of Ophelia, floating on the river. Ophelia does not follow the current, but goes upstream to the source.

The music becomes more and more metallic. The Mother changes into Ophelia, and as beautiful as she, rises toward the light.

The Testament
Ōno is happy to find his mother in Ophelia. He wraps himself in a huge white cloth: it is his mother he is carrying on his shoulders.

Before dying, his mother had whispered to him in her delirium: "A flounder is swimming within me." It is the dance of this fish that he wishes to relive. Together they turn towards death. He carries his dying mother in his arms or on his back. Over and over, they cross the border which separates life and death, and as the music becomes gentler, they walk together towards rebirth.

This first part is highly abstract. The dancer is but a body responding to the transformations of his inner being. Sometimes his entire action consists of listening. Sometimes he repeats a gesture with the obstinacy of an insect. Or he struggles like a blind man in a forest of vines. It is a fleeting world where forms never take root.

In a second version (in order to make the highly abstract first part more accessible), Ōno included some of the images from "The Dream of the Mother" (a sequence from his performance "Ozen"). In this second version, he wears a red kimono, and dances with the little ozen table to the *shamisen* tune "Rokudan" that his mother liked to play.

In the second part, entitled "I Can Never Give It Back," he is an adult. Dressed in a black suit, he expresses his gratitude toward his mother to the strains of "Liebestraume" by Liszt. "I live with all the unpardonable errors that I have committed. Thank you. Forgive me."

His work becomes only form and expression. He leaps on stage, eyes wide open, like a child, or a Pierrot, lost in a fairy-tale world. At the end, he improvises freely to Chopin's "Etudes."

In this section, Ōno gives birth to his mother, just as his mother gave birth to him. He carries her in him as she carried him. Life has come full circle. Man has created woman as woman has created man. And everything rests on the original duality, this eternal cycle in time and in flesh. Finally, he summons all mankind and the history of humanity.

Ōno's mother.

Family picture, Ōno (left) in his teens.

Dead Sea

During his tour of Israel in 1983, Kazuo Ōno discovered the Dead Sea. This marked the beginning of another long reflection on life, death, and birth which culminated in the creation of his most prodigious work.

This dance piece takes place in whiteness: the white of salt, of light, where human passion leaves its mark or is lost forever.

The stage is covered with a white carpet, and bordered by huge cream colored panels. Ōno, wearing a white gown and cape, slowly explores this immaculate world, then strides across it as if to take possession. The gestures of the first part, "Invitation," remain close to the body, slow and tense. White on white: the cosmos and the beings who inhabit it are one; the fetus and the mother are one; the cycle of the generations is but the perpetuation of life and of light.

The second tableau, "Requiem," passes like the wind of madness. Dressed like a wandering prophet, he dashes on stage and flings himself about like an oracle possessed. Carried away by the march played by a brass band, he cries out his rage and his joy of life. He covers himself with a white veil and passes among the audience. "Thank you. Arigatō. Gomennasai. Pardon me," he says, before being caught up once again by the sound and fury of the tragicomical stream of life.

Following this great outburst, his son, Yoshito Ōno, appears in a ray of light, frozen like a statue. It is a moment of rest, a long breath; as if we were bending to touch the earth . . . the salt, as if we were listening to the wind blowing across the Dead Sea.

Then, with large, all-encompassing gestures, Ōno appears to embrace the entire universe, and to play with matter. This tableau is "An Episode in the Creation of the World."

"Deserted Garden" is tender and gentle. Ōno seems to be engaged in a lovers' dialogue, amazed by what surrounds him.

Yoshito Ōno then brings us back to the reality of the immutable desert, eternally arid. He marks huge circles on the stage, slow swirls of sand on the dunes.

Finally, we have "The Ghost and the Viennese Waltz," veritable fireworks where Ōno reveals his entire art. Dressed in black, he dances wildly. Now a child, now a puppet, despairing or overcome with joy. But never alone. He always seems to be speaking to someone. The audience? God? Just as in the finale of "Admiring La Argentina," he offers us a hymn to dance and to love.

"From time to time an unknown being appears and disappears casting a light like salt."

"The dancer's costume is to wear the universe."

Yoshito Ōno

"The dead start running . . . ."

"Steps of the dead carrying love, bewilderment of the dead searching for love."

A Class with Kazuo Ōno

A class with Kazuo Ōno is no ordinary class. When does the class begin? When we take the train from Tōkyō to Yokohama? When we climb the path which leads to his house on a hill? While we sit around the table in his studio, drinking tea and listening to him before beginning work?

Sitting cross-legged in his armchair, he speaks. "My art is an art of improvisation. It is dangerous. To succeed, one must first reach the very depth of the human soul, and then, express it..."

He says that he doesn't like to teach, that he doesn't know how. And this is true. He doesn't "teach." He nourishes; he guides; he provokes; he inspires. This is undoubtedly the difference between a "master" and a "teacher."

The class begins. He assigns a subject for improvisation. The "dead body" is a theme he often suggests. "What could be the life of that which is dead? It is this impossibility which we must create." He explains that for his dance, we must not try to control the body, but to let the soul breathe life into the flesh.

He adds: "Be free! Let go!" Being free is not doing what we want or what we think. On the contrary, it means being liberated from thought and will. It means allowing life to blossom within. "You are happy because you are free. You smile: a flower blossoms in your mouth."

He approaches a student who is holding his arms above his head. He indicates the limits of space thus formed and tells him, "There is an entire universe here." He then adds, "Paradise is at your fingertips." To another he hints, "I am glad to be alive!" Then for all to hear, "You are glad to be alive!"

He later explains that the illogical is liberating, that the impossible opens new paths. "Today, you will dance Hamlet in a world of frogs."

Although he will sometimes correct a pose or explain the elementary movements of the body, he generally avoids imposing the slightest technique; it is up to the student to create whatever techniques are necessary. Ōno is there to open up the imagination, to help discover the soul. He guides the student so that he may become like "the creator of the world, he who has no identity, he who existed before the appearance of the individual. Then, all is but a game."

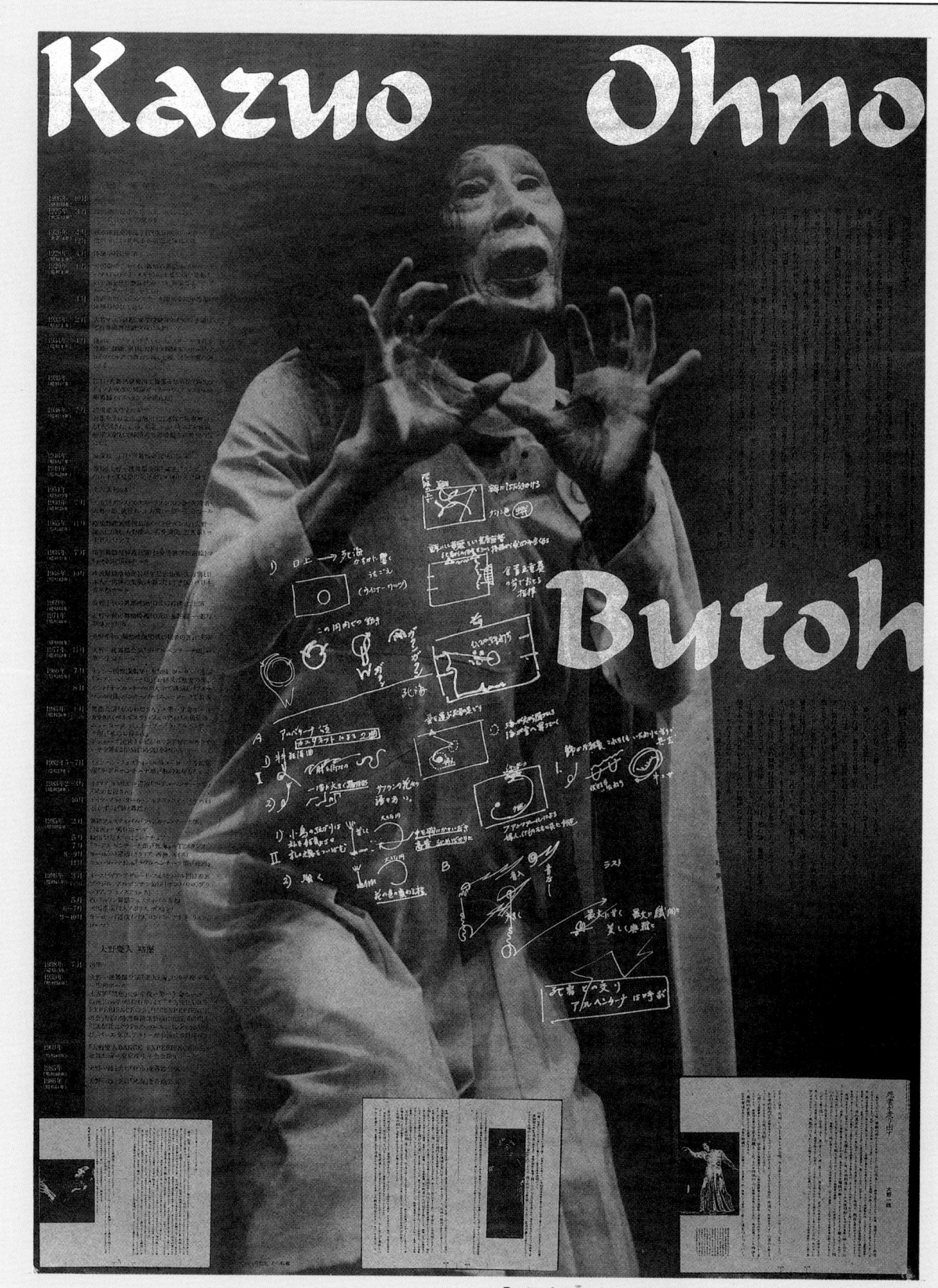

Poster for Ōno's retrospective performances, Yokohama, 1986

Poster for "My Mother," Tokyo, 1981

Poster for "La Argentina," Tokyo, 1977

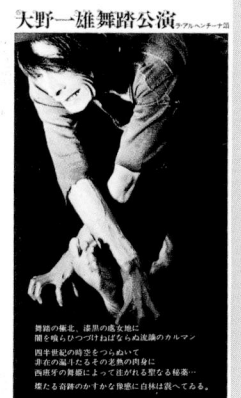

Poster for "Dance Experience," Tokyo

Ōno and Hijikata

CHAPTER II

TATSUMI HIJIKATA
THE ARCHITECT OF BUTOH

(Biography written with the help of Asbestos Theater, Mr. Nario Goda, and Ms. Kazuko Kuniyoshi)

1928 Born in Akita, Northern Japan.
1959 "Kinjiki" (Forbidden Colors)
 "Cheering Woman"
1960 "Bride"
 "T. HIjikata Dance Experience No. 1"
 "Saint Marquis—Dance of Darkness"
1961 "Secret Ceremony for an Hermaphrodite"
 Performance Ankoku Butoh-ha (Dance of Darkness School) in Ōsaka
1962 "With the Group of Leda"
1963 "Anma" (Masseurs)
 "Bara Iro Dance" (Rose-Colored Dance)
 "Illustrated Book of Sexology Instruction—Tomato"
1967 "Keijijogaku" (Emotion in Metaphysics), for T. Takai
 "Butoh Genet" for "M. Ishii Dance Experience"
 "Kamaitachi", photography collection by E. Hosoe. Performs "Neko" (Cat) in "O Genet" by M. Ishii
1968 Choreographs Y. Ashikawa's first performance
 "Neko (Cat)—A dance to pinch a fish, a dance to eat rice from a cauldron"
 "Tatsumi Hijikata and the Japanese—Nikutai no Hanran" (Rebellion of the Body)
1969 Produced several short pieces introducing Y. Ashikawa and S. Kobayashi
1970 "Hijikata Collection"
 Performs in "Honegami Toge Hotokekazakura"
1971 "Bai-Love," "Susume-dama," etc.
1972 "Nagasu Kujira" (Fin Whale)
 Tōhoku Kabuki: "Shiki no Tame no 27 Ban" (27 Nights for Four Seasons), "Hōsotan" (Story of Smallpox), "Susame-dama," "Gaishiko" (Study of Insulator), "Nadare Ame" and "Gibasan."
1973 "Shizukana Ie" (Calm House)
1974 Started the group Hakutōbō with Y. Ashikawa. Produced "Hokutōzu," Bijin to byoki," "Ebisuya otchō," etc. (16 pieces in two and a half years)
1977 Directed "Admiring La Argentina" for K. Ōno
1978 "Fortnight for the Louvre Palace—12 Phases of Dancing Princess of Darkness" for the exhibition "Ma—Espace/Temps" in Paris.
1983 Published the book *Yameru Maihime* (Hakuisha Publishing Co)
 Directed "Hook Off 88—One Ton of Coiffure in Scenery"
1985 "Tōhoku Kabuki Project" 1–4
1986 Died at the age of 57

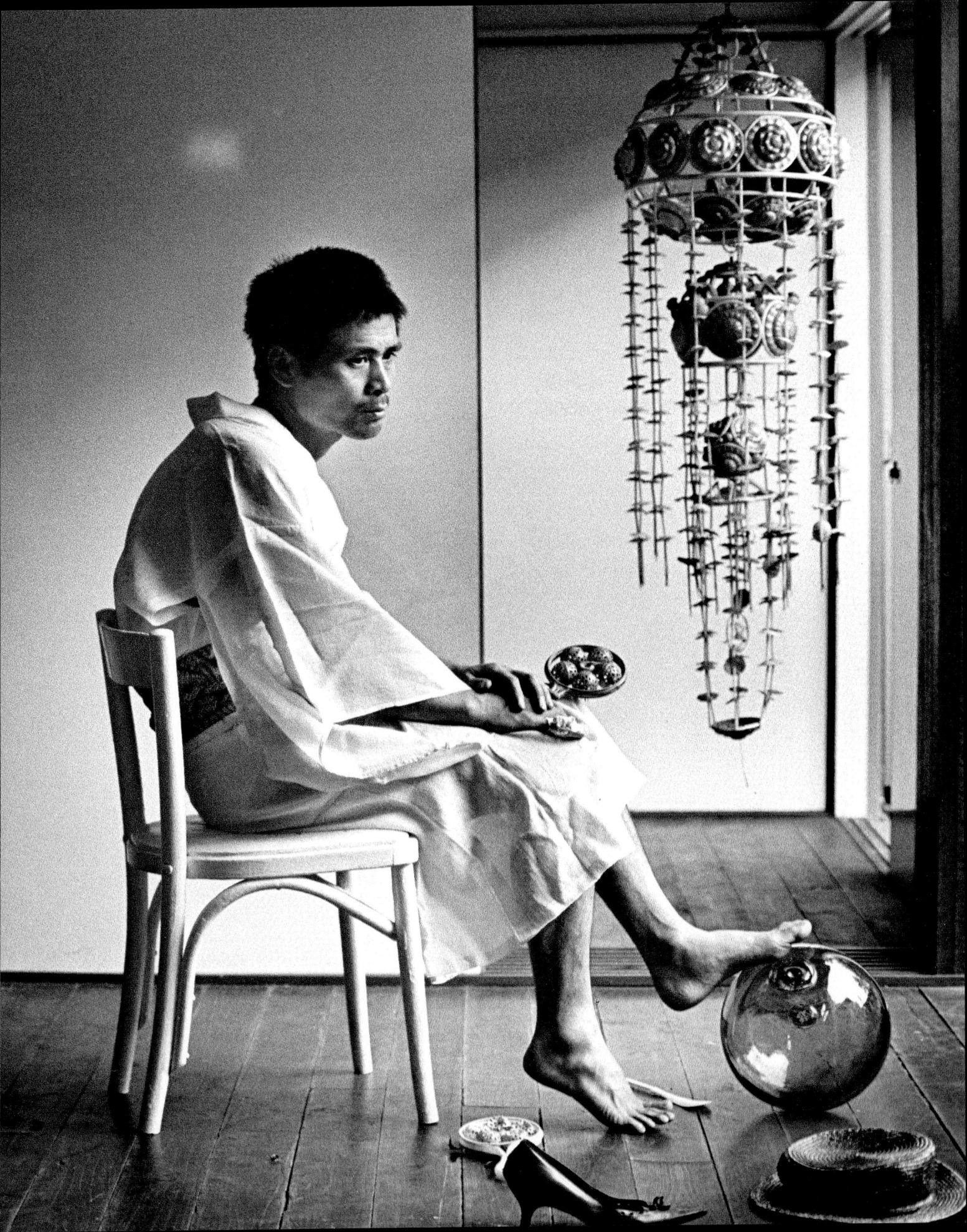

"Mr. Tatsumi Hijikata has just secretly informed me that he will once again celebrate an heretical ceremony. I look forward to attending it, and for the occasion am preparing a black mask and mysterious perfumes for myself.

Classical and avant-garde literature are in a state of crisis. But I can always find a symbolic, modern language in his work." Yukio Mishima

If Kazuo Ōno is the soul of butoh, then Tatsumi Hijikata is its architect. It is through his work, his story, that the awareness of butoh came into being. He defined the limits, the principles and the directions; he stated the aesthetics and created the techniques necessary for its development.

Rebellious by nature, he understood how to take advantage of his enormous energy and his capacity for self-examination in order to shake up the rules, turn the obvious upside-down, and transform the accepted idea of what dance was.

A night person, Hijikata spent his evenings in bars, and between performances of his pieces had the members of his troupe dance in the night clubs he owned. He thus upset the well-mannered aesthetics of the dance world by projecting into it the aggressive and vain night club universe. The world of the night remained essential to his work. His imagination never ceased to draw from it, and butoh carries the unmistakable mark of this alternate universe of darkness, confused sexuality, phoney eroticism and artifice.

Hijikata's influence extended beyond the dance world. An impressive personality, he became the pole of attraction toward which were drawn the greatest painters, musicians and poets of the sixties, as well as activists such as members of the Zengakuren, a radical student movement. All were fired by the energy and creativity of Hijikata.

Beginnings

Tatsumi Hijikata forged the concept of Ankoku Butoh (Dance of Darkness) after undergoing far-reaching upheavals in his artistic outlook. These occurred in progressive stages, generally preceded by periods of silence and introspection.

In order better to understand the basis upon which his butoh was built, it is essential to look at the various dance pieces which mark Hijikata's artistic experience.

Like Kazuo Ōno, Tatsumi Hijikata began by studying modern dance. He took classes with Kazuko Matsumura (herself a student of Takaya Eguchi who was a disciple of Mary Wigman) in Akita, and later, in Tōkyō, Hijikata pursued his study of modern dance with Mitsuko Ando.

In 1956, he danced under the name of Kunio Hijikata in the second show of M. Ando and K. Horiuchi's "Unique Ballet Group." He participated in their third show in 1957, and in 1958, under the pseudonym Tatsumi Hijikata, he was the assistant choreographer for a short dance piece, "Haniwa No Mai," part of a festival organized by the Association for Contemporary Performing Arts. This marked the end of his contribution to modern dance.

Tatsumi Hijikata's true debut occurred on May 24, 1959, during a series of performances organized by the Japanese Dance Association. He performed a short piece inspired by a novel by Yukio Mishima: *Kinjiki* (*Forbidden Colors*). This piece created a scandal, and several members of the association threatened to resign should similar pieces be sponsored in the future.

The violence of a young artist aware of his difference and determined to disregard anything outside his experience and to overcome any obstacle to the development of his art, was already visible in Hijikata's "Kinjiki."

More than a creative work, it was, in fact, a venture in

destruction, a monument of rebellion through which Hijikata hoped to forge a new path for his dance.

In this piece a young man (Yoshito Ōno) has sexual relations with a hen, after which another man (Tatsumi Hijikata) makes advances to him. There is no music. The images are striking: the young man smothers the animal between his thighs to symbolize the act.

There is nothing reminiscent of any particular dance technique, but the piece already displays the fierce desire to transform the body which forms the basis of Hijikata's further experimentation with technique. Hijikata conceives of dance as the need to break through the shell formed by social habits, which keep the body lagging behind the revolutions already accomplished in contemporary thought. For him the body is not a means but an end, not to be used to transmit ideas, but on the contrary, to question, to rethink, to recreate. Dance is not a linear composition, not a syntactical arrangement of body movements, but rather the exploration of the exemplary depth of the body itself; not a desire to pronounce a discourse, but to search for meaning.

During the four-year period which separated "Kinjiki" from "Anma" ("The Masseur," 1963), Hijikata's choreographies were essentially inspired by the works of such writers as Mishima, Lautréamont, de Sade, and Genêt. In his work he probed the world of eroticism and violence. In sexual perversion, he found a key to the depths of the human body and thus a means to develop his art. His study of the transformations experienced by the body when its most hidden levels are revealed allowed him to form the basis of a dance of "being" rather than "appearing."

Thus the name "Ankoku Buyō," (Dance of Darkness), which he chose in 1960 for his dance form. He wished to express in his work the most obscure facets of the personality. His discovery of the techniques for transforming the body, necessary to reveal its authenticity, were later to lead him to change the term "buyō" to "butoh." This choice was an affirmation of the differences which separate his work from that of traditional Japanese or Western dance forms.

Hijikata aspired to infuse his works with ceremonial form, an aspect of heretical ritual which gave the powerful impression of exerting an influence on the imagination of his audience. (There is an apparent hint of the mark left on him by the *kagura* dances of his childhood in the Tōhoku district.)

Among the choreographies created during this period, most noteworthy are "Divine," danced by Kazuo Ōno, as well as "Maldoror" and "The Secret Ceremony of an Hermaphrodite."

"Butoh plays with time; it also plays with perspective, if we, humans, learn to see things from the perspective of an animal, an insect, or even inanimate objects. The road trodden everyday is alive . . . we should value everything."

"My mother used to say, 'Run with the heart of the blind.'"

After "Anma," the references to literary works disappeared and Hijikata turned toward more specifically Japanese themes. In "Anma," particularly, he appeared in a white kimono on a stage covered with tatami mats, accompanied by the music of the *shamisen*.

The wearing of a kimono allowed him to rediscover the archetypical forms and gestures of Japan. This was also true for the music and the sets. This claim to Japanese identity culminated in a performance in 1968 entitled "Hijikata and the Japanese—The Rebellion of the Body."

This piece left an unforgettable impression of uncontrolled savagery and destructive derision.

Hijikata enters the stage on a wooden litter carried through the audience by several men, followed by a pig in a baby crib, and a rabbit on a platter held at the end of a pole. The swinging of this makeshift palanquin, the movement of his white bride's kimono worn back to front, and the terror of the animals, all join together to bring the

spectator into a precarious, uncertain, and confusing world, where nothing appears to have a hold on reality. Once onstage Hijikata removes his white kimono, under which he wears only a golden phallus. He begins a barbarous dance, leaping suddenly onto immense metal plates suspended from the flies, which fling light out in an image of unbound chaos, increasing the sensation of violence. In the end, with a reference to "Kinjiki," he kills a rooster by breaking its neck.

In the second part, where the grotesque opposes the ridiculous, he appears dressed in a huge gown with a white satin train, mocking Western ballroom dances, and taking a humorous stab at other conventional forms of dance.

He ends the piece spread-eagled by ropes which pull him toward the rear of the house, above the heads of the audience, this parody of the Ascension marking his farewell to the West.

"I am very aware that my butoh originates somewhere totally different from the performing arts related to religion—Buddhism, Shintoism or whatever—I was born from the mud."

72

"I keep one of my sisters alive in my body when I am absorbed in creating a butoh piece, she tears off the darkness in my body and eats more than is necessary of it—when she stands up in my body I sit down impulsively."

"When I begin to wish I were crippled—even though I am perfectly healthy—or rather that I would have been better off crippled, that is the first step towards butoh."

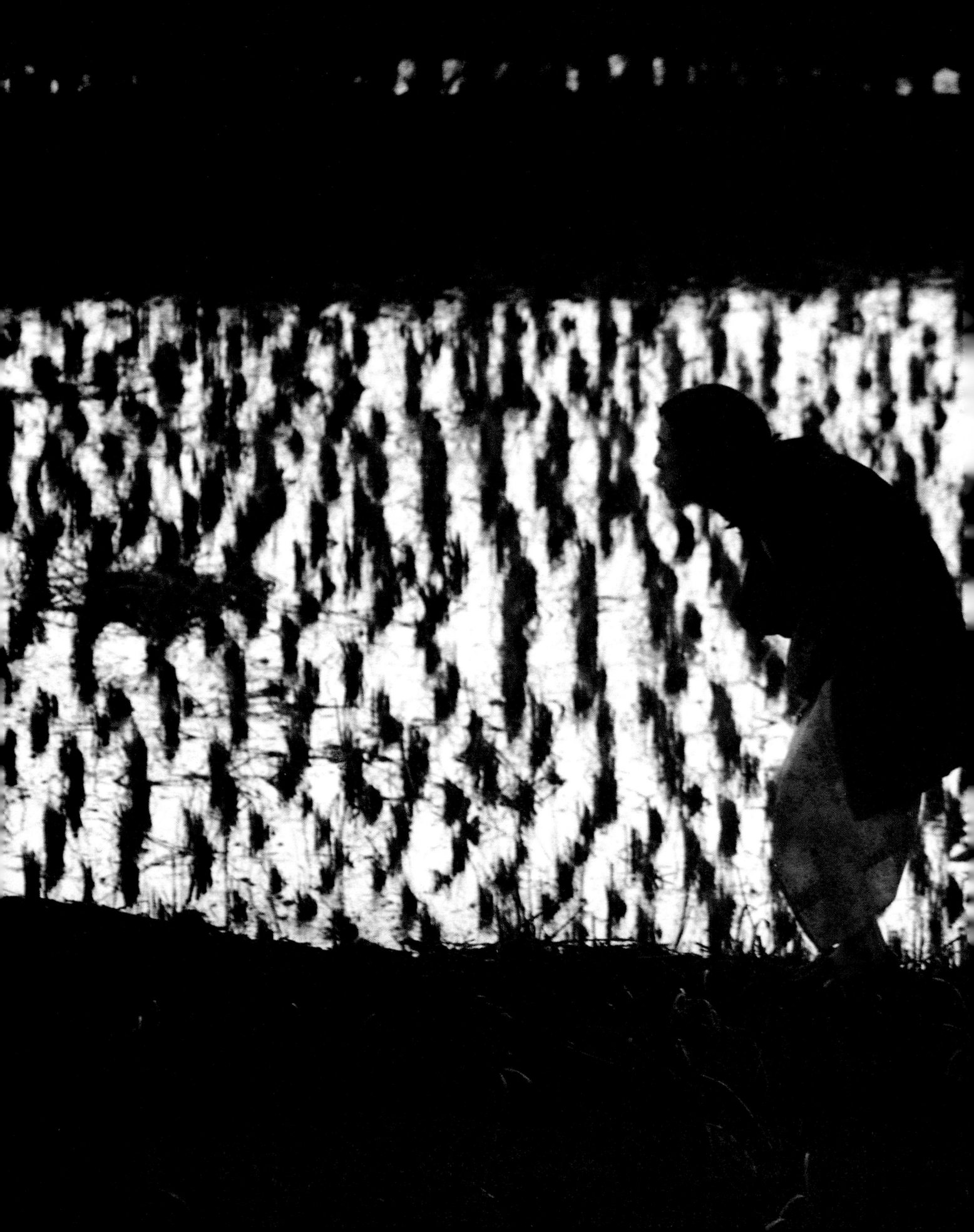

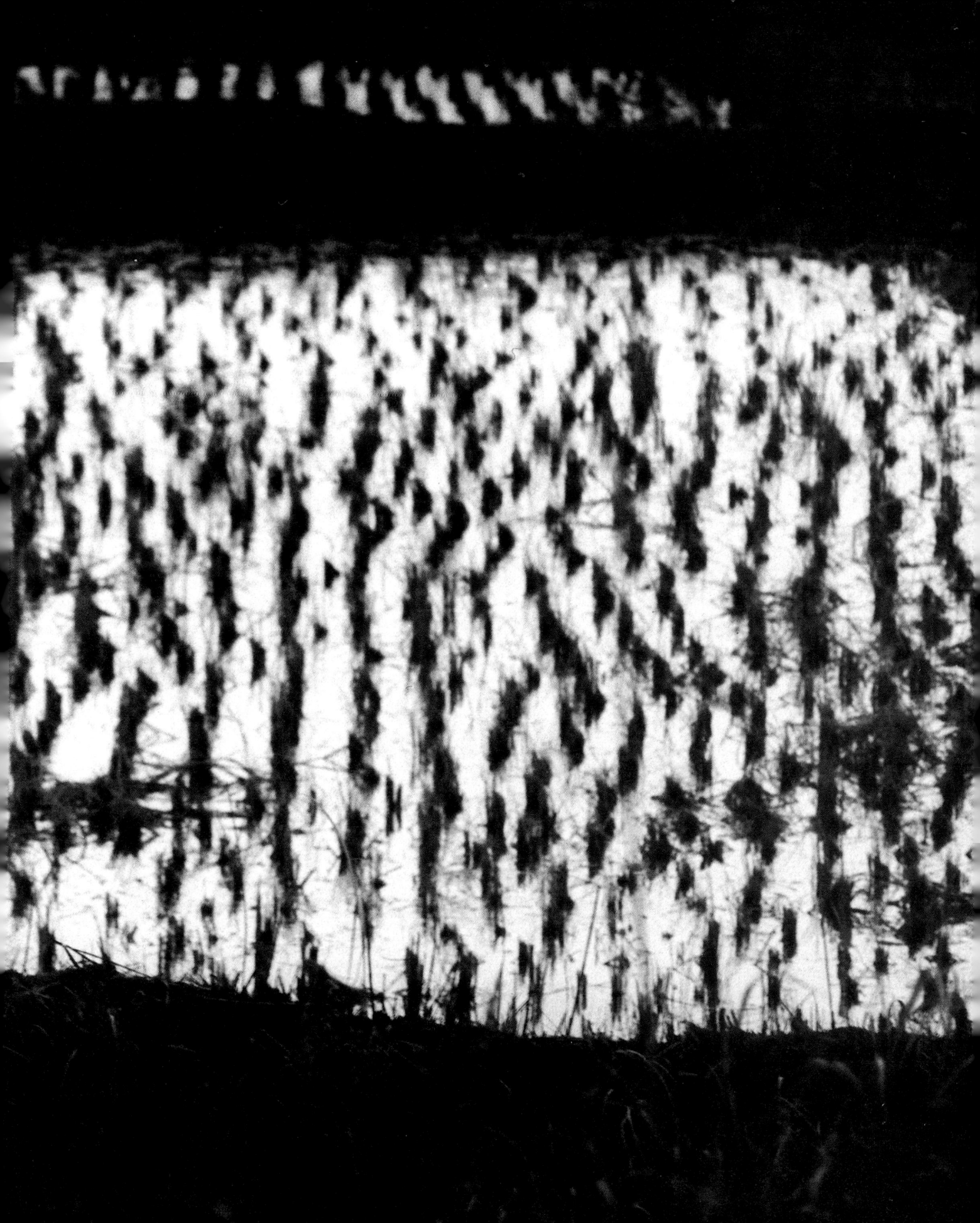

"... through dance, we must depict the human posture in crisis ..."

Hijikata and Ashikawa

Until then, Hijikata had worked primarily with men, including Kazuo Ōno and his son Yoshito, Akira Kasai, Mitsutaka Ishii and Kōichi Tamano. Butoh was associated with an essentially masculine world.

However, during the four years of silence which followed "The Rebellion of the Body", Hijikata's reflections on his roots and his family, as well as his encounter with Yoko Ashikawa and Saga Kobayashi, were to prompt him to transform his dance profoundly.

A journey to his native village impressed upon him the need to return to the sources of his art, and his search for a Japanese dance was transformed into nostalgia for his origins. Little by little he acquired the conviction that his mother and his sisters lived on in him. He would often say, "My sisters, who were sold so that my family might survive, are within me. I nourish them in my body." This led him to meditate upon woman and the relationship of the feminine body with dance, meditations which consequently had an overwhelming effect on his creative life.

He believed that man, removed from earthy and maternal forces, possesses a "poetical" body—a body touched by the spirit and prisoner of the logical world.

Only woman has retained the carnal body, as yet unarticulated in language. "Women are born with the ability to experience the illogical part of reality and are consequently capable of incarnating the illogical side of dance. If we imagine that a man's body gathers itself around a center, then a woman's opens outward in an act of scattering of seeds."

It was at this point that Hijikata began working with three women: Yōko Ashikawa, Saga Kobayashi, and Momoko Mimura. In contrast to his earlier collaborators, they had no basic training in classical, modern or traditional dance. Therefore he had to create a technique which would enable them to deal with his choreographic concepts.

His work centered on having them try to uncover woman's original life force, attempting to master the body, overcoming their physiological limitations. They studied ways to bend the body to its limits, knees flexed, allowing total freedom of the ankles and neck. In order to crystallize and deepen the feeling of presence in the body, he avoided rapid and exaggerated movements, and kept very close to the ground, with the center of gravity very low in the pelvis.

"The Story of Small Pox," Kōichi Tamano in the center.

Yōko Ashikawa in Kyōto University event.

Hakutōbō

Hijikata continued his choreographic work with Yoko Ashikawa's essentially female troop, Hakutōbō, in residence at the Asbestos-kan Theater.

By then, Yōko Ashikawa had already mastered the techniques of metamorphosis and was attempting to widen the landscape between being and the "other," and to assume all its forms: wind, stone, young woman, cat, and so on.

In Hakutōbō's last show, "G Senjō No Okugata" (1976), the summit of butoh aesthetics and of Yōko Ashikawa's art, we see Yōko distend her body, distort her face, play with equilibrium and bend her body into the most incredible positions. She appears as a tiny dwarf, her body huddled, surrounded by giants; she performs a clownlike dance and turns herself into a witch. During a very erotic scene, her body becomes fluid, slender and light, hands flapping like butterfly's wings or like a nest of agitated snakes.

Following that performance, Tatsumi Hijikata remained in the background until 1983. He did, however, choreograph Yōko Ashikawa's solo, performed in Paris at the Autumn Festival of 1977, and for the exhibit "Ma-Space/Time."

Alone on stage, accompanied by silence or the music of a *koto*, she changes substance—now flower, now stone, now water—endlessly creating a multiple and polymorphic body in a mysterious ceremony never to be forgotten by the few spectators fortunate enough to have witnessed it.

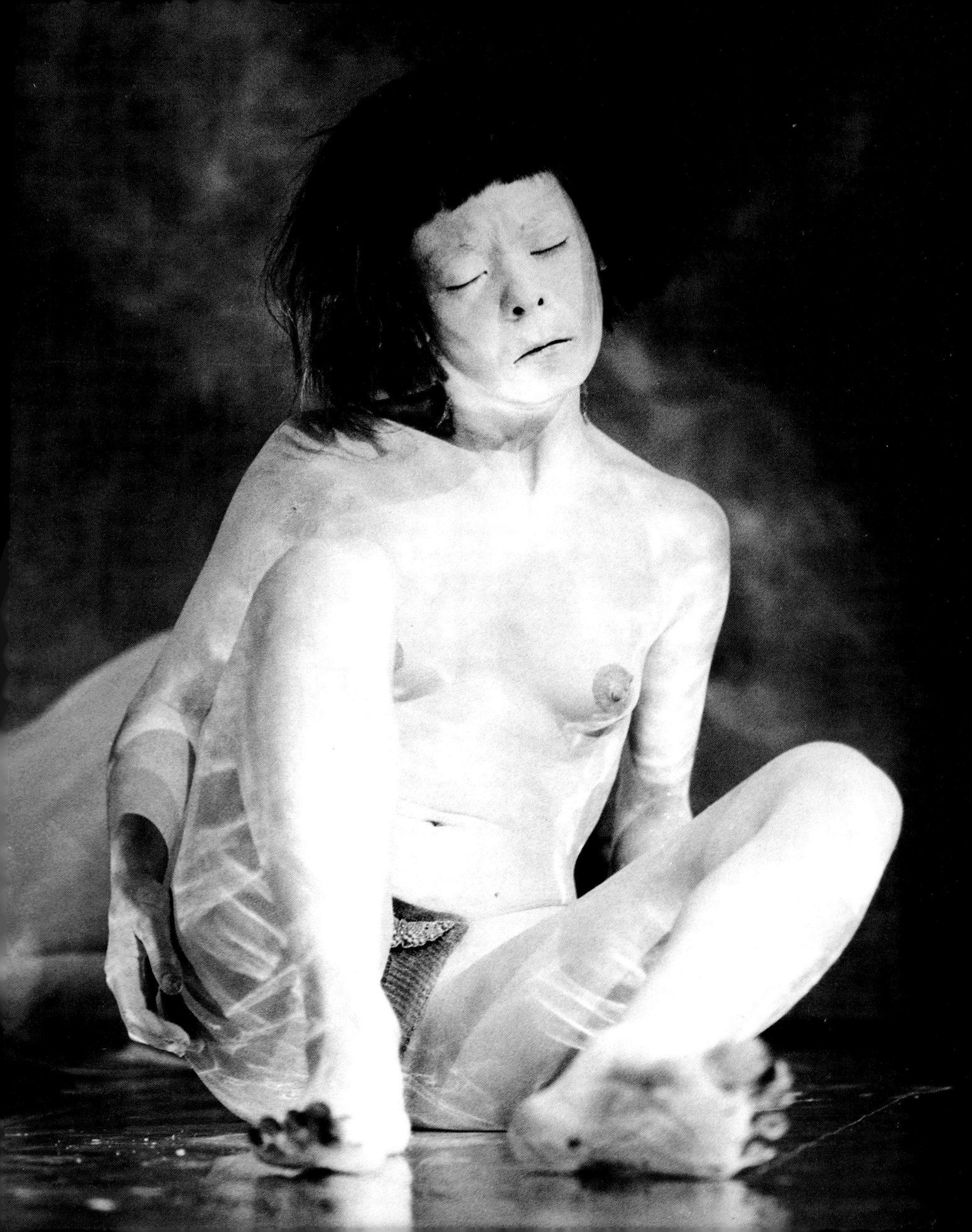

The Return of Hijikata

In 1977, Hijikata collaborated on the choreography of Kazuo Ōno's first version of "Admiring La Argentina." During the years which preceded his return to the limelight of butoh, Hijikata continued his work with the Asbestos-kan, trained dancers and remained in the wings pulling the strings of the movement which had begun to break out of its limited sphere. He wrote, and devoted his nights to managing his night clubs. In 1983, however, he was encouraged to make a comeback. He organized a film and slide program of his past work. Then, in April, he presented three pieces with Yōko Ashikawa, resulting in "The Breasts of Japan," which toured Europe.

From the catalogue for the 1960's E. Hosoe movie, "The Navel and The Bomb."

Min Tanaka's Maijuku Group at the Butoh Festival, 1985, in a dance choreographed by T. Hijikata.

Those in the audience familiar with Hijikata's work were on the whole disappointed. The energy and depth of his past performances were nowhere to be found.

Tired old whore, geisha's ghost, doll, grimacing monster, frightened aborigine, clay statue... Yōko Ashikawa had lost none of her talent; she continued to transform herself endlessly as she had in the past. Somehow, though, none of the magic was visible in the performance, only the effort that had gone into its creation. Perhaps too much was expected from Ashikawa's comeback. Had her image been blown out of proportion by the memory of the past?

Hijikata's choreography for the Hoppō Butoh-ha group and his collaboration with Min Tanaka on "Foundation" in 1984 were met with similar disappointment.

Hijikata seemed unable to abandon his earlier creations. Perhaps this difficulty in renewing his art was indicative of the dead end which the butoh movement had reached. Perhaps, experimental work on the "regionalization of the body" (that is, specific physical characteristics dependent upon the local culture in which one is raised) cannot develop beyond the particular in order to reach the common base of humanity in the service of a more universal art, thus remaining only within the exotic.

Hijikata's desire to create new forms had led him away from the original vigor of butoh, dance of "being," whose truest expression is found in the freedom of improvisation. In his desire to enrich butoh, had he somehow lost its prime energy, its vital strength? Had the forms destroyed the being; had he closed behind him the very doors he had once opened?

Nevertheless, in the series of performances, "Tōhoku Kabuki," with Yōko Ashikawa and a new troop of young female dancers which he formed shortly before he died, Hijikata revealed a new tendency toward abandoning the spectacular and flashy techniques, concentrating instead on the expression of life and of being. Unfortunately he did not have the time to develop this new approach fully.

Until his death in January, 1986, Hijikata remained the sufficed to inspire the dancers, and his criticism and advice constantly stimulated and guided their work, as well as their lives. He considered butoh his personal territory and was vigilant in his desire to see it remain worthy of his image of it. Everyone feared his comments, and came to him when in difficulty. His death left a vacuum in the world of butoh which is hard to fill, and the doubts expressed in reference to his work seem to vanish when we

"A La Maison de Civeçawa," poster by Tadanori Yokoo, 1965

E. Hosoe Photo-exhibition, poster by Tadanori Yokoo, 1968

"Shizukana Ie," Tokyo, 1973

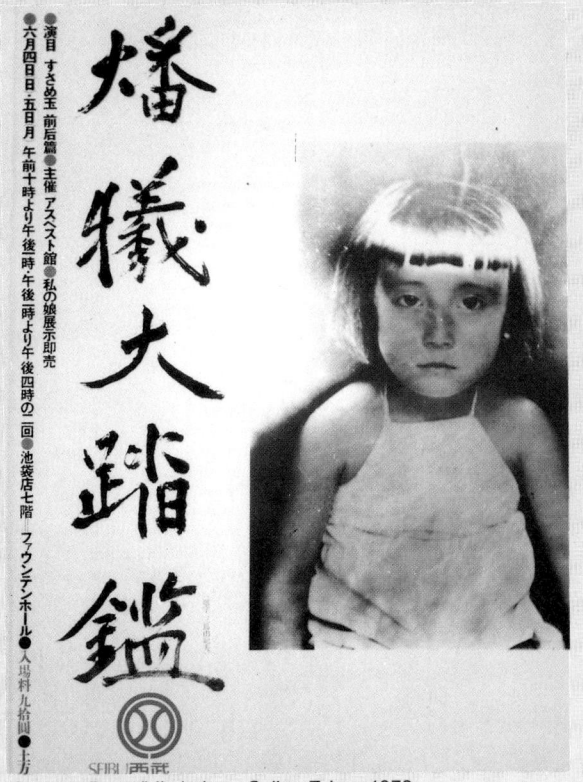
"Susame Dama," Ikebukuro Seibu, Tokyo, 1972

CHAPTER III
HIJIKATA'S LEGACY

Dairakuda-kan

1972 Establishment of Dairakuda-kan
"Dance Apricot Machine"
1973 "Ah Romance"
"Kinkon Bird"
"Phallus God Story"
1974 "Saint Testicles"
"Man Flesh Story"
1975 "Goldfish Plays God"
1976 "Storm"
1977 "Ivory Order"
1978 "Wind Inversion"
"Silent Head"
1979 "Head in the Fair Wind"
"Peoples Like Poor Pole"
1980 Series of "Lights" 1–6
"Sea Dappled Horse"
1981 "Block"
1982 "Susanō"
1983 "Melting Breeze"
1984 "Dawn of Japan"
1985 "Gorin No Sho" (The Book of Five Rings)
1987 "Rashōmon"
1989 "Kaidan," "Rashōmon"

Sankai-juku

1975 Establishment of Sankai-juku
1977 "Amagatsu Shō," (Hommage to Ancient Dolls) Ushio Amagatsu Recital
1978 "Kinkan Shōnen" (Kumquat seed)
1979 "Sholiba"
1981 "Bakki"
1982 "Jōmon Shō" (Hommage to Prehistory)
1984 "Netsu no Katachi" (Shape of Heat)
1986 "Unetsu" (The Eggs Stand Out of Curiosity)
1988 "Shijima"

Tōhō Yasōkai/Byakko-sha

1977 Creation of Tōhō Yasōkai
1980 Creation of Byakko-sha
"The Forest of Hidden Screams"
"The Grand Ceremony of Golden Fish"
"The Forest of Whales' Bones"
1981 "Shōnen Shōjo no Kusudama"
1982 "Nap on the Grass," "Silent Pleasure"
1983 "Sky Lark and Lying Buddha"
1984 "Television like Minakata Kumakusu"
1990 "The Book of Deads"

Dance Love Machine

1975 Establishment of Dance Love Machine
1979 "Revenge of the Toad"
1980 "Frankenstein's Octopus"
1981 "Le Con de la Renarde"
1982 "Flesh," "The Trial of Love," "Girl of Fire" series, "Le Prince des Sots"
1983–4 "Detarame" series
1985 "Softly as in a Morning Sunrise," "Musical Potlatch" series
1986 Berlin Festival "Kibunteki"
1987 "Doctor Notenki I & II," "The Sea of Romanoff"

Kō Murobushi/Sebi

1967 "Kiku", "Cancan", "Celebrating M. Monroe"
1970 "Yamabushi"
1976 Establishment of Sebi, "Komusō"
1978 "The Last Eden" (Sebi and Ariadone)
1980 "Lotus Cabaret," "The Mummy" (solo)
1981 "Hinagata VII—Neon or Nought" (solo)
1983 "Iki" (solo)
1985 "Outside" (solo), "Ko Wandering Body," "Mr. Kafka"
1986 Creation of the Company Kō Murobushi "Pantha Rei," "The Tears of Eros"
1987 "HoH"
1988 "Ephemere"
1989 "Mayu-ka" (solo), "The Cycle of Stupor"

Carlotta Ikeda/Ariadone

1974 Establishment of Ariadone
1975 "Female Volcano"
1976 "The Blue of the Sky"
1977 "Tattoo"
1978 "The Last Eden" (choreographed by Kō Murobushi)
1980 "Zarathoustra" (choreographed by Kō Murobushi), "Lotus Cabaret" (with Sebi)
1981 "Utt" (solo, choreographed by Kō Murobushi)
1985 "Hime" (The Princess)
1987 "Chiisako" (The Spirit of the Young Child)
1988 "Black Grey White"

Muteki-sha

1968 "Bicycle Race," choreographed by T. Hijikata
1969 "Portrait of Reiko"
1972 "Summer Holiday"
1973 "Extract from Hinemosu Kagurazaka"
1976 "It was just to be like this night," directed by T. Hijikata
1977 "Van Gogh Eulogy"
1982 "The Garden"
1987 "Sleep and Reincarnation—From Empty Land"
1990 "Ghost Story" (Homage to Lafcadio Hearn)

Yōko Ashikawa/Hakutōbō

1967 Maiden Recital
1970 Genjusha performances series
1972 Appears in "Twenty Seven Night for Four Seasons" directed by T. Hijikata
1973 Appears in "Calm House" directed by T. Hijikata
1974 Establishment of Hakutōbō
1974–76 Yōko Ashikawa dances in all 13 works of Hakutōbō directed by T. Hijikata
1978 Solo dance for Paris Festival d'Automne: "Twelve Phases of the Dancing Princess of Darkness—Fortnight for the Louvre Palace"
1983 Dances in "The Breast of Japan" directed by T. Hijikata
1985 Dances in the "Tōhoku Kabuki Project" I-IV directed by T. Hijikata
1986 Hakutōbō reforms
1987 Performance series "Skin Clock for those wishing to become a dog," "Construction Site Salome" (T. Hijikata Memorial Performance)
1988 Hakutōbō performances: "Nichirin", "Getsurin", "Karin", "Nyūshoku no Onna," "Shiumu—Yōko Ashikawa and the Japanese"
1989 Hakutōbō performances: "Yameru Hichō", "Hifu-uchū no magudara", "Kaze ni Yorisou Onna"

Butoh-ha Tenkei

1981 "Hakuchi Gun" (The Idiot)
1982 "Noichigo" (Wild Strawberry)
1983 "Zakuro Tan" (The Birth of a Pomegranate)
1984 "Usagi no Dance" (Rabbit Dance)
1986–87 "Humoresque 1–5"

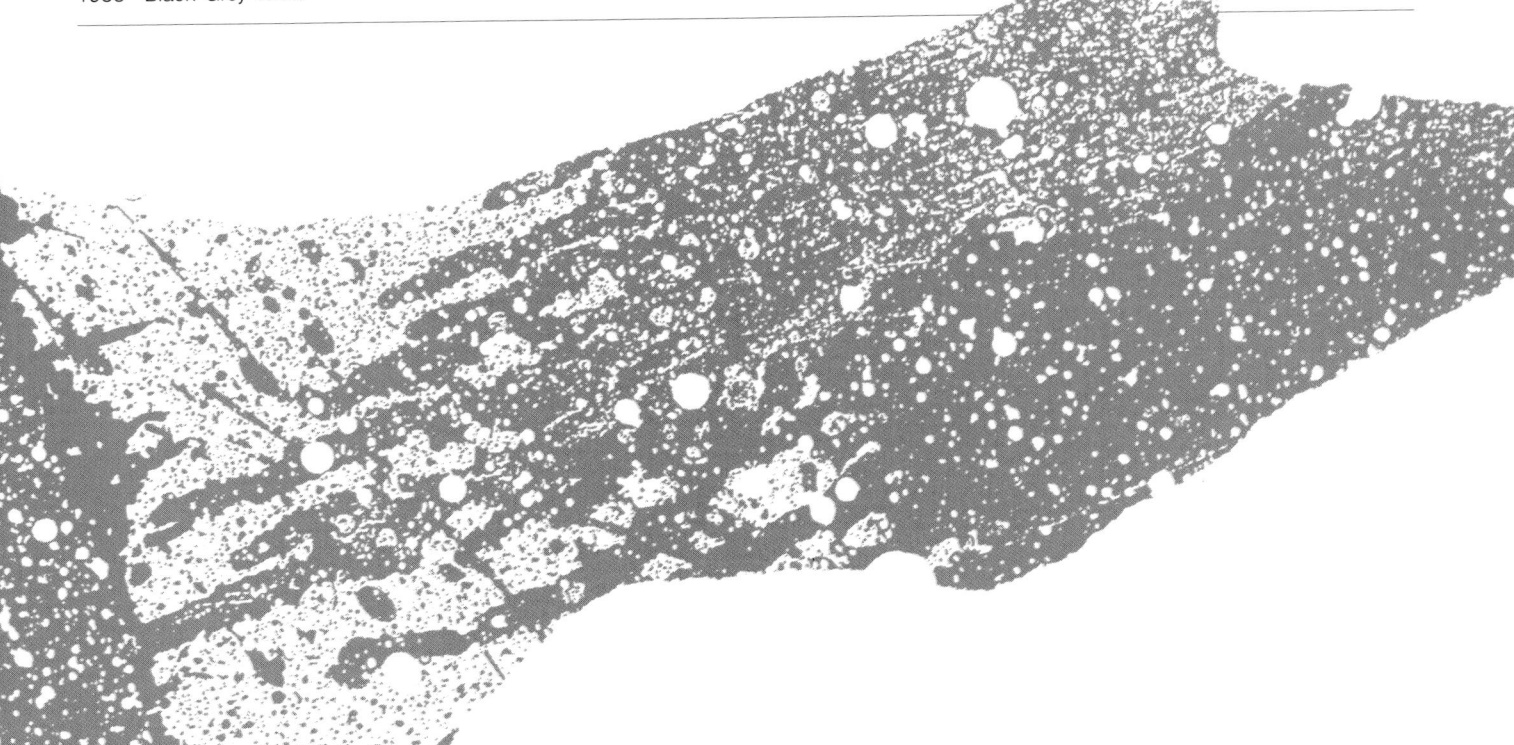

A number of companies followed in Hijikata's footsteps and it is essentially through their work that butoh is known abroad.

A formal style of butoh has emerged with a recognizable technique, but which endlessly repeats identical images and staging, combining enticing exoticism, the parody of rituals, and heretical images, attempting, in vain, to provoke shock or surprise.

Faithful to the principles of Ankoku Butoh, the performances of these companies might almost be considered as "image factories." Their basic tenet of refusal sometimes loses its meaning and impact, however, becoming a purely aesthetic tool, and the systematic rejection of discourse often conceals a lack of any real point of view. Nevertheless, the standard themes of butoh are present in these performances: nostalgia for pre-modern Japan, poverty (the use of tattered kimonos, planks of wood for the decor), playing with androgeny or excessive eroticism, depersonalized man, tortured bodies, surrealism, the desire to serve as society's foil, the taste for violence and the aesthetics of horror.

With this revival of Hijikata's version of butoh (sometimes an exact copy), there is no noteworthy evolution as far as technique is concerned. One is witness, rather, to decadence, the staging clearly taking priority over the dance itself.

Despite a lack of expressive originality, the spirit of revolt is still very much alive in these performances, demonstrating the sense of helplessness and confusion of young Japanese living in a society which has sacrificed both its culture and its lifestyle upon the altar of unrelenting materialism and economic well-being. It is this inner violence, the frustrations of an entire people, which explode on stage in a profusion of dream-like images, both horrific and fascinating, where a parallel, underground world comes into being: the universe of their fantasies, fears, desires and failures. Beyond the grating images of anger and the sumptuous representations of dreams, these performances are above all an attempt to exorcize their impotence.

Dairakuda-kan

Dairakuda-kan was the first company to be formed in the spirit of Hijikata's Ankoku Butoh, and remains its most important proponent to this day.

The Dairakuda-kan experience is not only artistic, but communal in spirit. In searching for an alternative within the world of dance, the company sought to establish a new relation to society. It is because of this daily-life experience

that their performances have such a vital, scathing, and authentic quality.

The director of the company, Akaji Maro, was a disciple of Hijikata. Originally a stage actor with the Budōkai group and at the Jōkyō Gekijō, he created his own company in 1972 with its first show, "Dance Apricot Machine." Although his first choreographies, such as "The Story of Human Flesh," or "Saint Testicle" in 1974, were created strictly according to the dictates of Hijikata, Akaji's theater background gave him a taste for the spectacular and an exacting sense of detail. Perhaps this explains his preference for images over dance itself.

When the company was first formed in 1972, it was comprised of excellent well-trained young dancers (Ushio Amagatsu, Bishop Yamada, Tetsurō Tamura, Yuko Yuki, among others) and the energy of their performances was

"Kimono have been used in Japanese theater before, but we moved away from what was considered beautiful and chose to use kimono with the cotton stuffing coming out . . . discarded things that were ugly and dirty."

the result of a dynamic group spirit.

Dairakuda-kan created many productions: "Goldfish Plays God" (1975), "Storm" (1976), "The Ivory Order" (1977), while performing with other companies at the same time. They achieved fame in 1978 with "Wind Inversion." In 1979, they presented "Head in the Wind" and "People Like Poor People." In 1980, they gave an important series of performances—"The Twelve Lights"—the full realization of Akaji Maro's baroque imagination. In 1982, Dairakuda-kan gave a number of performances in Tōkyō and Yokohama before embarking on a tour including the United States and an appearance at the Avignon Festival in France, where they performed a selection of their most successful pieces.

By the late 1970's, most of the best dancers had already left the company to establish their own groups: Amagatsu with Sankai-juku, Ōsuka with Tōhō Yasōkai, Bishop with Hoppō Butoh-ha, Tamura with Dance Love Machine, Yuki with Suzurantō, Murobushi with Sebi/Ariadonne, Tōri with with Tenkei-sha, Shimada with Taiyō Shinkan, and others.

The Dairakuda-kan which European audiences first saw in 1982 seemed rather like a decadent music hall entertainment—even the numerous group scenes, deafening music, and some occasional strong images were unable to mask the lack of content. The most recent performances by Dairakuda-kan in Tōkyō (especially at the 1985 Butoh Festival), despite some very impressive images and a powerful soundtrack, have only confirmed this unfortunate development.

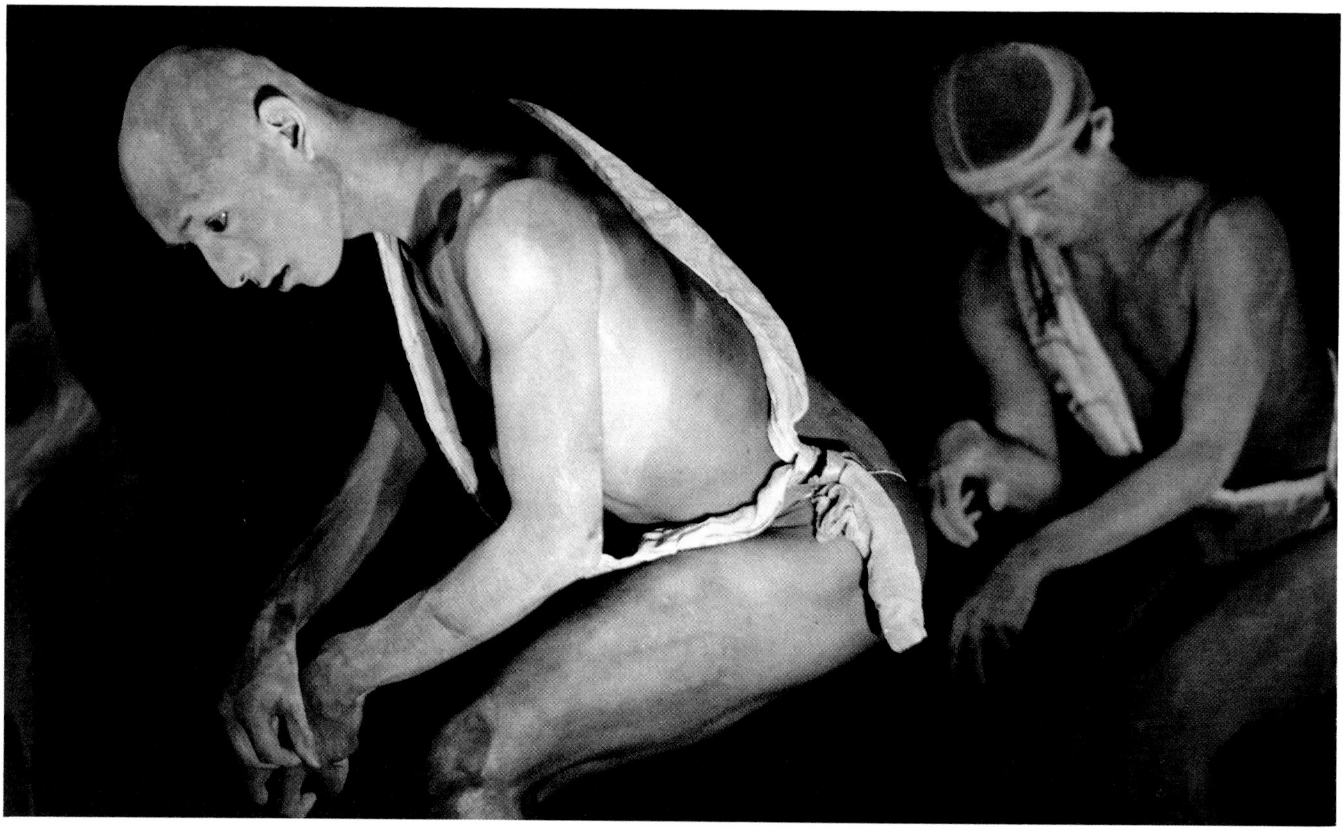

"I will put a sweet-potato on each seat of the theater. Some people might throw them at the stage, some performers might eat them on the stage ... Anyway, the theater must be fulfilled with sweet-potatoes. It's going to be a flood of sweet-potatoes." A. Maro

Sankai-juku

The spectacular group, Sankai-juku, is undoubtedly the best example of a contemporary, post-Hijikata butoh company.

The group's founder, Ushio Amagatsu, began his training in classical and modern dance before becoming involved with butoh. After working with Dairakuda-kan, he formed his own company in 1975 with three other dancers: this was to become Sankai-juku. (Later, in 1979, a fifth dancer joined the company.)

Their company's first performance, "Amagatsu Shō" (Hommage to Ancient Dolls) in 1977, was followed by "Kinkan Shonen" (Kumquat Seed) in 1978 and "Sholiba" in 1979. In 1980, the latter two were presented at the Festival of Nancy in France. Since then, the group has been based in Paris, and has toured throughout Europe and the rest of the world. "Bakki" was added to their repertory in 1981 and "Jomon Sho" (Hommage to Prehistory) in 1982.

Of all the leading companies which have followed in Hijikata's footsteps, Sankai-juku alone has moved away from the established pattern. With his highly aesthetic choreographies, Ushio Amagatsu has pushed his dance toward greater plasticity within an increasingly luminous universe. Butoh's physical technique has been made to serve surrealism, leaving aside Ankoku Butoh's obsession with violence and horror.

Sankai-juku's latest performances are accompanied by original music—oriental percussions, such as Yas Kaz, as well as the electronic music of Yo-ichiro Yoshikawa—which, together with the delicate beauty of the images, reinforce the artistic unity of the work (often lacking in other groups which generally use an assortment of different types of music).

Sankai-juku's imagination is fed by a kind of human archeology: "We are reaching for the origins of being. The vast chaos, so confusing, so marvelous. Our legs move, as do our fingers, and our entire body is in motion. It is the history of our existential origins which we interpret on stage."

Ushio Amagatsu

"Our performance, a collage of various moments, actions and spaces, becomes a ceremony. But it is all of these elements put together (dancers, audience, sound, lights) which place this ceremony in a shadowy world. Coming to the theatre and taking one's seat is already a ceremony. The human elements are not the only participants: the theatre itself is part of this ceremony; full-empty-full... it is in constant motion."

Their universe is often seductive or erotic, a mixture of archaic or ritualistic images. An officiant dressed in white blows into a conch shell while a cluster of naked men in white make-up, hanging by cords attached to their feet, slowly descends from above the stage, the sensuous, fluid dance of fish-men, the love-battle of naked warriors, a dwarf hops about before disappearing into the light....

The aesthetic sophistication developed in their earlier works was pushed to the extreme in "Unetsu" (The Egg Stands Out of Curiosity) (1986). In this mysterious ceremony at the edge of the water, ghostly beings endlessly collapse and arise, timeless, between life and death, the priests of a strange religion arrive striking gongs in a long incantation to an unknown god, and the snake man awakes from a long sleep to dance an infernal hymn to life.

Contrary to other butoh companies, Sankai-juku manages to create the illusion that the world it presents to the public exists independently of those who perceive it. The stage becomes a vast place of secret rituals which the audience attends without ever being solicited or abused.

Some critics consider this highly sophisticated approach (supported by every aspect of the staging, especially the lighting and music) to be a watered-down version of butoh, while others consider this to be its greatest achievement. In either case, Sankai-juku has been able to accept outside influences and has managed to evolve towards increasingly professional performances. As a result, the troupe has attained a greater world-wide success than any other butoh group.

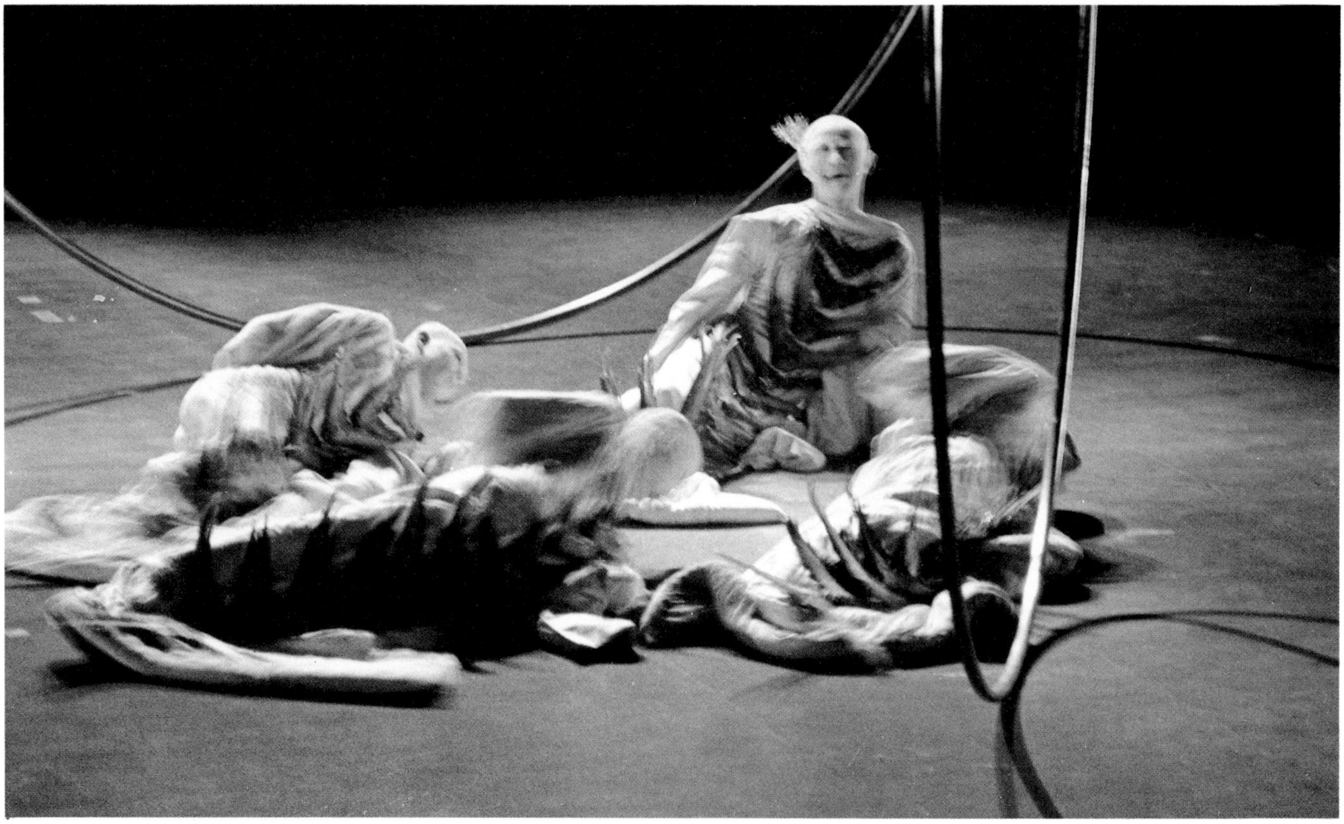

111

"When I say wind, I can imagine several kinds of wind. It won't be pantomime but the wind will emerge from inside the body." U. Amagatsu

115

Byakko-sha

The Kyōto group, Byakko-sha, founded by Isamu Ōsuka, is a community of thirty people living in a former factory. The company's work goes beyond the sphere of dance and reaches out into the plastic arts, not only through its work with sets and costumes, but also through the staging of actual living tableaux which are created on a given theme each time the company travels abroad—"The Last Supper" in Israel, "The Fashion Show" in Bali, or "Alice's Series" in Taiwan. The photographs taken of these events are as much part of the company's work as the performances themselves.

Byakko-sha always creates a festive rhythm for its performances. The group of musicians, Marupa, forms an integral part of the company, composing and playing explosive music which floods the stage with chaotic and catchy sounds.

As opposed to the rigor and refinement of Sankai-juku, Byakko-sha carries us into a Dionysian world hungering for total anarchy. The dancers invade theater and stage accompanied by cymbals and drums, like medieval players entering a village square. They create extravagant choreographic games, grotesque, provocative and extremely spectacular, in a clown-like universe, erotic, joyful, colorful. Rabbits hop around the dancers, watermelons are tossed about, and the audience participates in the fun.

In the midst of all this confusion, Ōsuka wanders in, like a bawdy king laughing at his lost majesty. The shamanic priestess of the group is the incomparable Hiruta Sanae, whose gestural language is rich and varied. Her solos are the high point of these performances: appearing first as a mummified idol, she gradually awakens, ending in a diabolic dance, like a fury, voluptuous and terrifying.

"Gourmet" series

"Encounter with the Caterpillar" from "Alice" series

Sanae Hiruta

"The Last Supper" at Dead Sea

"Eve in the Future"

"Hibari to Nejaka"

Isamu Ōsuka

Dance Love Machine

Dance Love Machine's performances use nonsense to the best advantage, often with very impressive staging. Dancers dressed in kimonos covered with studded plates go through the audience brandishing torches over their heads; a man leads a group of bare-chested women by a leash, whipping them as they walk on all fours; a depraved looking man performs a disturbing "masturbation dance"... Anzu Furukawa brings to the group her own sense of humor and subtlety, elements often lacking in butoh. Their work has recently become theatrical, heralding new dimensions for butoh.

In 1986 A. Furukawa separated from the group. She established the "Dance Anzu School" where she trains young dancers and performs. Tamura continues to choreograph Dance Love Machine.

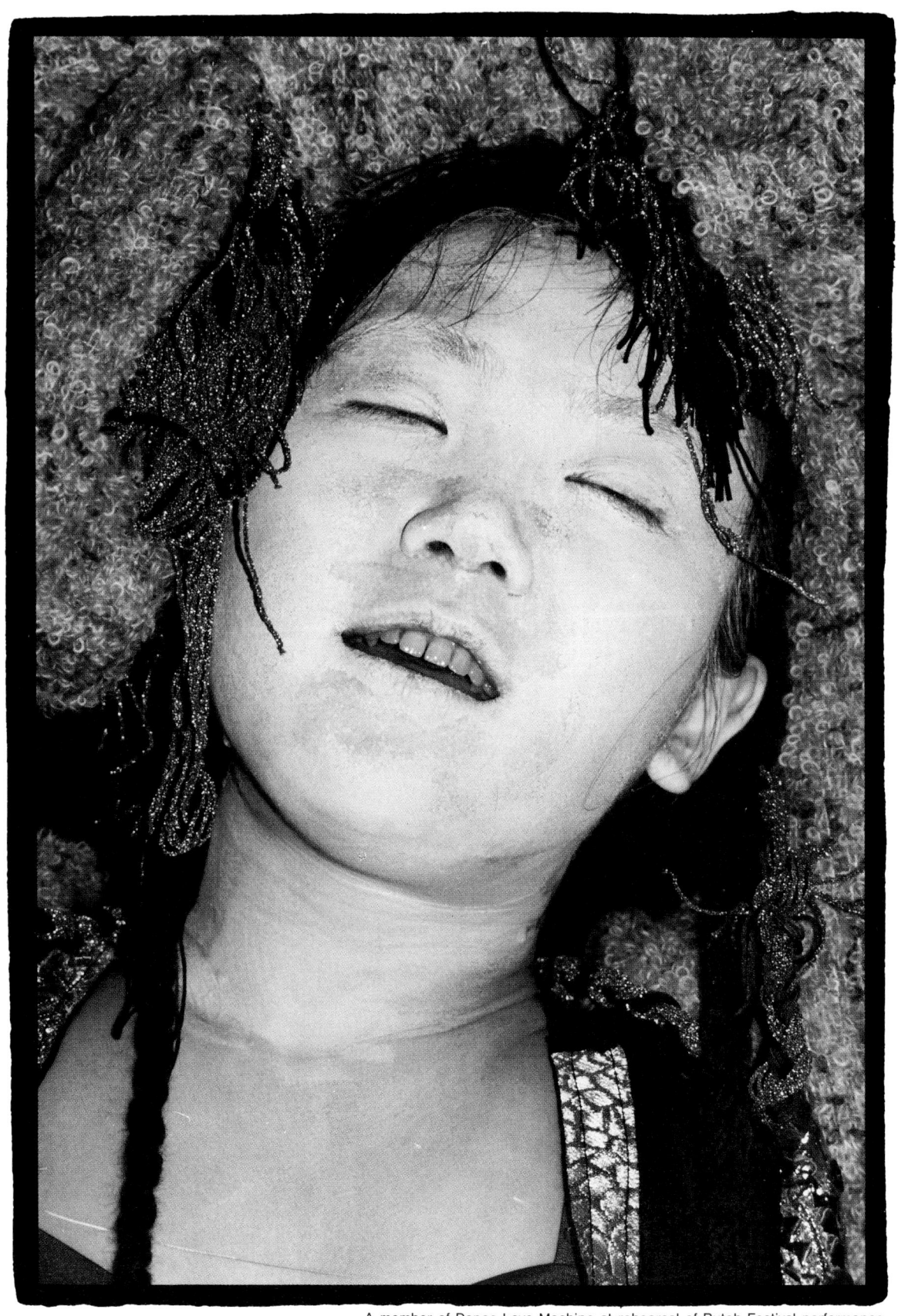

A member of Dance Love Machine at rehearsal of Butoh Festival performance.

Sebi and Ariadone

Kō Murobushi and his group Sebi concern themselves primarily with suffering and the ambivalence of life and death, the two extremes which perpetually feed each other. He has also done choreography for Carlotta Ikeda and her female dance company, Ariadone.

Like Sankai-juku, Carlotta Ikeda has settled in Europe and directs her research toward a more "international" type of dance. In her performances—notably "Zarathoustra" (1980), and her solo "Utt" (1981) which toured all over Europe—she explores the origins of life as well as the feminine world and the eroticism specific to it.

"My coccyx is longer than normal (a bit like prehistoric man's) and I have flat feet. Yet, even as a child, I dreamed of becoming a dancer. It wasn't necessary, however, to be reborn in order to have a dancer's body, for I really loved my flat feet and my coccyx. In fact, I think my eroticism comes from that.

"In 1973, covered with gold powder and with a phallus fastened to my waist, I made my cabaret debut. I performed a belly dance. The phallus vibrated and my coccyx accentuated the fullness of my buttocks. The shaking evoked sexual ecstasy.

"This first experience has remained profoundly engraved in my body. I'm still not sure that my first performance wasn't a kind of trap, yet, knowing it might be, I still took the train to Hokkaido.

"I was trapped in any case. Since then, I continue to cry out the action that penetrates deeply within me, to the ends of the earth, to the far reaches of the unknown, to the unfathomable depths. My destiny as a dancer is represented by the eroticism of my flat feet and my coccyx."

Speaking of her work, she adds, "For me, dancing is rediscovering the life process, experiencing the intensity of existence with a finer notion of time. While dancing, I gradually become aware of an inner world, of another "me," and my butoh is enriched by this new universe which I have discovered."

129

Sebi

Ariadone

Muteki-sha

Natsu Nakajima was born in 1943 on Sakhalin, north of Hokkaido. She studied classical and modern dance in Tōkyō from 1955, before encountering the work of Ōno and Hijikata. Although she was impressed by the teachings of Ōno, Hijikata was to become her intellectual and choreographic guide. In 1969, she founded a small company, Muteki-sha, whose performances were often directed by Hijikata. In 1982, she premiered in "Niwa" (The Garden) with Lili Maezawa, her protege. Between 1983 and 1986 she toured Europe, the United States and Israel with this production. "Niwa" is a single life-long project expressing the continuity of the dancer's existence.

Hijikata's influence is manifest in her highly structured performances. These are a mosaic of the varied and contradictory fragments of her personality and express the development from dream to nightmare, from purity to darkness.

"Niwa is a forgotten garden, very tiny, very Japanese: it is the garden of my memory of childhood. I wanted to see my life from the perspective of a woman seated in a garden, watching it bloom and wither."

The impact of this work derives entirely from the way she uses her body on stage. A giantess is born of a dwarf, as the adult is born of a child—the infinitely big of the infinitely small. The child's dream becomes the adult's nightmare. The energy shifts between the seasons of space and those of the body—an energy heavily charged with a nostalgia for times that have been and times to come. Imagination and memory stimulate the vital impulses of the flesh, and her dance is born of existence itself, beyond a specific form or imagery.

"I want to find a balance between the animal and the spiritual, between what is revealed and what is hidden. Also I want to move people, of course, to provoke and touch them with my dancing, but above all, to communicate a sense of humanity."

"We human beings belong to the world of nature as intelligent beings, but at the same time we have to live like animals. We must live with this reality which is part of contemporary society. Hijikata always said that in dance the body must move with life—not only show the spiritual side, but also the energy of death, of sex, of life consumed in joy or sorrow. I want to free the body of its inhibitions."

"Butoh should reject any notion of symbolism, message, or formalism, and only express its energy and freedom. It is not art that I aspire to, but love."

"Hijikata would tell us: 'Make the face of an old devil woman, with the right hand in the shape of a horn, and the left hand holding her long hair' . . . .
Then comes the light of the sun, and the eyes become smaller; then comes the wind, and the eyelids quiver; then you must feel like a stone . . . and the body must react each time to these stimuli while keeping the same basic movement."

Natsu Nakajima and Lili Maezawa.

Hoppō Butoh-ha and Suzurantō

Bishop Yamada was among the founders of Dairakuda-kan, after having studied and performed with Tatsumi Hijikata. He created the group Hoppō Butoh-ha in 1975, and then retreated to northern Japan (he finally settled in Otaru, at the northern part of Hokkaido) in search of Japanese primitive culture (because the north of Japan was the last place to receive Japanese culture).

He also directed performances by the group of female dancers Suzurantō, founded by Yūko Yuki.

He moved back to Tōkyō in 1984, when he performed "Takazashiki" (The House of the Falconer) (choreographed by Hijikata) and has directed a butoh school in the suburbs of Tōkyō since then.

Two People for Three Nights

After Hijikata's death, Yōko Ashikawa went on working with the group of dancers who had been studying with Hijikata at the time.

This group started to perform in 1987. The performances of Two People for Three Nights, directed by Yōko Ashikawa, evoke a delicate, feminine and nostalgic atmosphere, in a world of memories and dream.

We should also mention the group Taiyō Shin-kan, who ceased their activities in 1980; the group Butoh-ha Tenkei, founded in 1981, which creates a quiet and poetic world in their performances; the work of several solo dancers: Man Uno, whose work is similar to performance art; Moe Yamamoto, a student of Hijikata who created his own group in Kanazawa; Kōichi Tamano, who worked with Hijikata in his early performances and is now settled in the United States; Tomiko Takai, one of the first female butoh dancers (she appeared in several performances by Hijikata) who has recently started working independently; Goro Namerikawa and Kenichi Morita, both of them dancers from Sankai-juku, who now create their own solos.

Kōichi Tamano

Tomiko Takai

Gorō Namerikawa

Mutsuko Tanaka of Tenkei-sha.

Yōko Ashikawa

Dance Love Machine's pamphlet for "Le Con de la Renarde," 1981

From Dairakuda-kan's catalogue, 1987

Sankai-juku's poster

Sankai-juku's poster

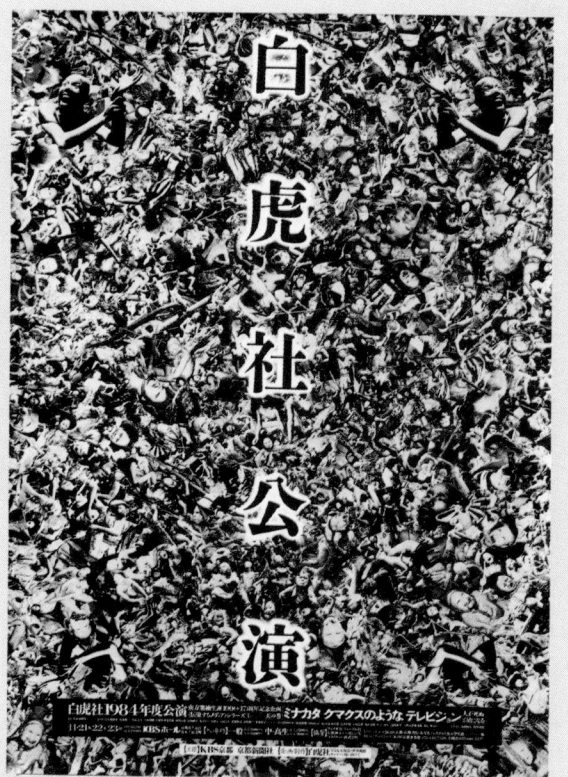

Byakko-sha's poster, "Skylark and Lying Buddha," 1986
Designed by Tsunehisa Kimura

Byakko-sha's poster, "Television Like Minakata Kumakusu," 1984
Designed by Tsunehisa Kimura

Yoko Ashikawa's pamphlet "Skin-clock for Those Wishing to Become A Dog," 1987

"The Violent Season" News Paper introducing first members of Dairakuda-kan, 1974

Ariadone's poster featuring Carlotta Ikeda

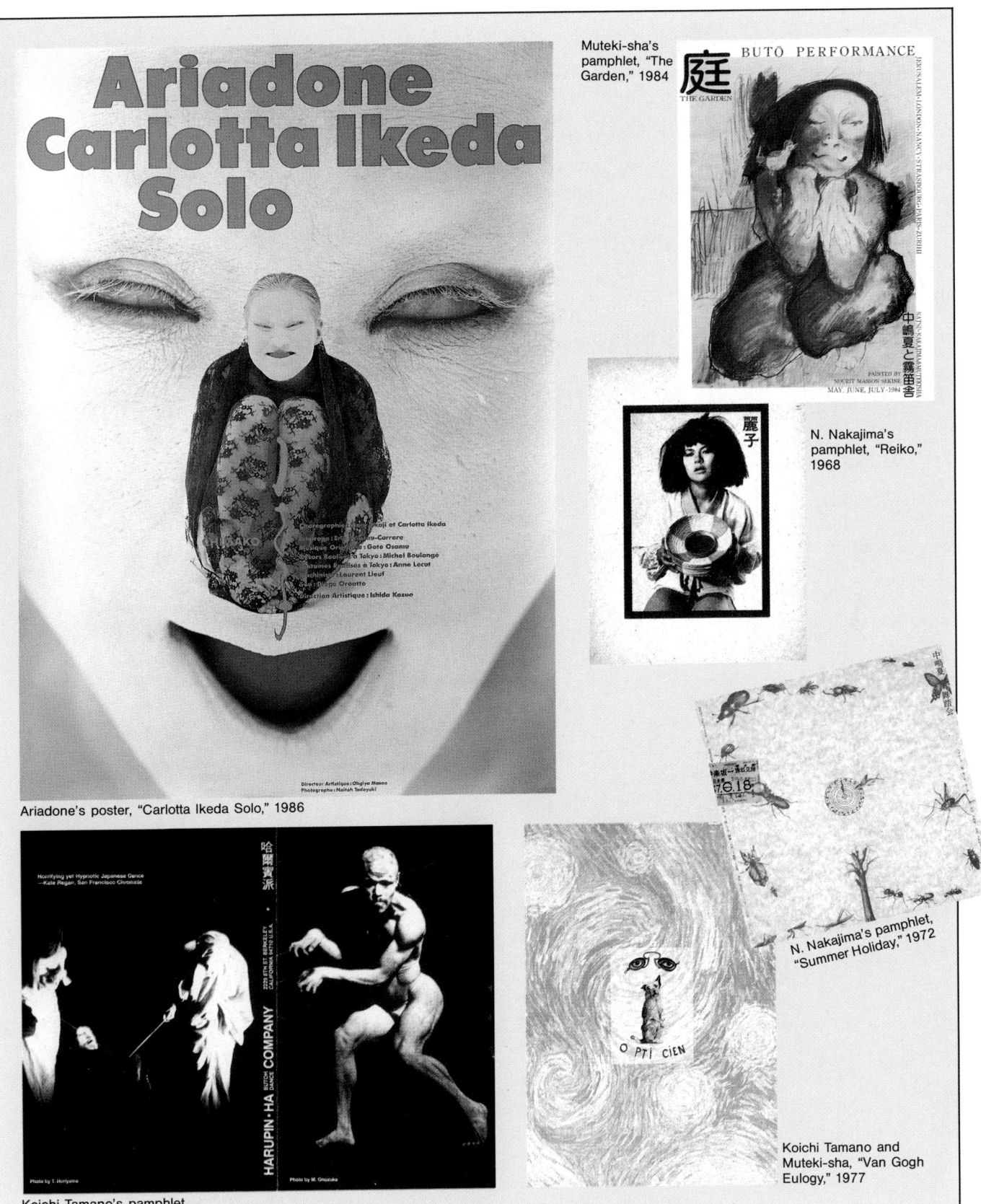

CHAPTER IV
IMPROVISATIONAL BUTOH

Akira Kasai/Tenshi-kan

1967 First recital
1969 "Tannhauser"
1971–72 Establishment of Tenshi-kan, "Down the Hill," "Tannhauser II"
1973 "Seven Seals"
1974 "Requiem for Amaterasu," "The Gate of Initiation," "Illusory Garden"
1976 "Future of Material," "Tristan and Isolde"
1977 "Queen of Pluto"
1978 "Universe of Ethel" series
1979 "Akira Kasai Butoh Pieces" series, End of Tenshi-kan
1980 Akira Kasai Last Butoh recital

Mitsutaka Ishii

1967 Butoh Genêt
1968 ô Genêt
1969 Butoh Ichi (Butoh Market)
1977 Mu-Dance (Dance of Nothingness) series
1982 Jizai I (Freedom I) series
1983 Nigari (Bitterness)
1984 Jizai II series
1986–87 Jizai III series

Min Tanaka/Maijuku

1973–75 Solo series "Subject"
1975–77 Solo series "Butai"
1977–81 Solo series "Hyper-Dance Drive"
1981 Establishment of Maijuku
1982–84 Solo series "Emotion"
1983 Duos with Yōko Ashikawa "Very Highly Air Absorbive Bromides"
1983–85 Solo series "Form of the Sky"
1984 Foundation of Ren-ai Butoh-ha with Tatsumi Hijikata; Performance of "Foundation", commemorating his 1501 solo (directed by T. Hijikata)
1985 "Moon in Daylight" with Maijuku
1986 "Investigations"
1987 "Can One Dance a Landscape?"
1987– Solo series "Diary"
1988 Choreography for "Carmina Burana"
1990 Choreography for the opera "Idomeneo" by Mozart; "The tree," "The Rite of Spring"

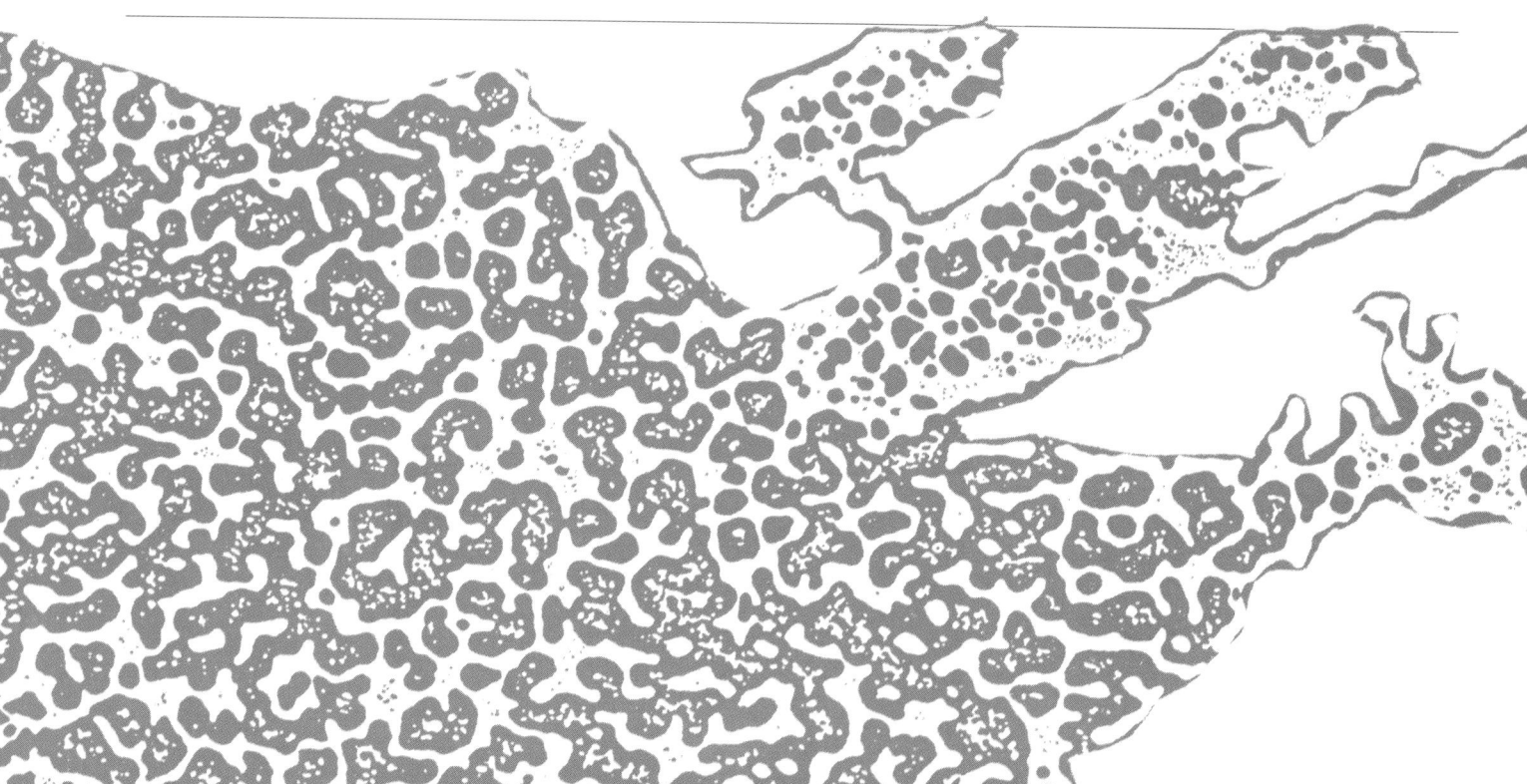

Whereas the Ankoku Butoh style that derived from Hijikata emphasizes the systematic construction of a specific universe, a formalized world and a particular gestural quality, there is another, almost diametrically opposed tendency, based on improvisation and the free expression of an inner universe.

It is in this type of dance that butoh's original vitality can still be felt. These dancers have avoided the trap of an established code of expression or of overly sophisticated productions. On the contrary, their goal is for the body to become the immediate voice of a spiritual or imaginary world. As such, their work often goes beyond the traditional notion of a performance, attaining an almost religious or metaphysical dimension.

This is true of Akira Kasai, around whom much of this type of dance crystallized before he himself stopped performing in order to dedicate himself to Eurythmics.

Akira Kasai

After studying classical dance, Akira Kasai became a student of Kazuo Ōno. He participated in some of the earliest butoh performances, especially Hijikata's "Pink Dance" in 1965. His first solo performances "Invitation to Dance" (1967), "The Child's Table" (1968), and "Tannhauser I and II" (1969 and 1972), were very much inspired by themes of androgeny, perversity, and eroticism.

Later, he was to lean increasingly towards Shintoist theology, the philosophy of Gurdjieff and occult thought.

In 1972 he established his own dance school, the Tenshi-kan (The House of the Angel). He created a number of performances with his students, especially "Down the Hill" (1971) and "The Seven Seals" (1973). From "The Gate of Initiation" (1974) onwards, the influence of Rudolph Steiner became increasingly apparent in his work. Finally, in 1979, he left Japan for Germany where he studied and now practices Eurythmics.

Basing his work on transformations of the body, Akira Kasai is unquestionably a butoh dancer, although he differs radically from Hijikata's Ankoku Butoh in his desire to reveal an inner universe. Whereas Hijikata emphasizes the importance of a tangible, structured form, Kasai, like Ōno, is interested primarily in sharing his inner universe by allowing consciousness to impregnate the body and give it the form it chooses. His dance is essentially the echo of impulses which stem from his inner world. He is not concerned with perfect expression, but rather wishes to dance the vital importance which he sees in the different layers of his most intimate being.

In this, he is more interested in an almost mystic revelation than in technical virtuosity. Thus his choreographies often appear somewhat chaotic if they are seen only as performances and not looked at in terms of their spiritual dimension.

Where technique is concerned, Kasai works less with curves and bending than do other butoh dancers, and he uses a center of gravity situated quite high in the chest area. For this reason his dance often appears less well-rooted, more fragile than that of others.

For his dances, he chooses a theme, decor, and music, and improvises within an extremely tight structure. Most of his performances are given only once.

More than his choreographies, however, it was his school, the Tenshi-kan, that was responsible for his influence. In addition to technical training, much emphasis was placed on meditation and personal development.

This may explain why a great many of those dancers most concerned with renewing butoh, yet retaining its essential qualities, are Kasai's former students. They form a "new generation of butoh."

"My overall perception is that the physical state of the body does not exist." A. Kasai

"Everybody is a dancer. A dancer is an angel who is corrupted and stands apart from everyday life. The dancer does not

choose to dance as one alternative in life, but is rather chosen." A. Kasai

Mitsutaka Ishii

Along with Kazuo Ōno and Tatsumi Hijikata, Mitsutaka Ishii is one of the pioneers of butoh. He has played an important role in furthering the style of butoh that stresses improvisation over formalized structure. Early on he produced his own pieces, including "Genêt" in 1967. In 1971 he left Japan for Europe where, aside from his performances, he organized a number of dance workshops. Upon his return to Japan, he performed in duo with his wife, Bettina Kleinhammes.

In his dance work, improvisation is used as a guerrilla technique. His anarchic, wild mind rejects any attempt to conceptualize butoh, nor is any concession made to the spectacular or to glossiness. In his art, as in his life, he refuses anything conventional.

To Ishii, the location of the performance is unimportant. It might take place anywhere: in a park, a bar, in a reception hall or a temple. He considers dance to be an act, not a performance. In order to establish clearly his independence from Hijikata's Ankoku Butoh, he calls his work "Mu-dance" (Dance of Nothingness). He is perhaps the only dancer for whom butoh's original flame of rebellion, fired twenty years ago, continues to burn. For this reason he is an unusual artist, undefinable and disturbing, a conscience lost in the heart of the butoh movement.

"Repeating a specific form," he says, "or simply transmitting it, cannot give birth to a profound meaning. Only the essence makes the form significant. The dancer must discover how to become one with his own forms.

"The controlling and checking of one's ego and emotions represent a new point of departure towards a personal process of organic growth.

"Just as sound is born of silence, calm envelops all movement. The being within the total void allows the body to discover the new strings which will move it.

"Meaning does not arise from concepts, but is reflected by the movement, for both the audience and the dancer.

"Music is not meant to fill in or to illustrate. Sound and music are direct and spontaneous; they provoke impulses, actions and reactions, which reflect the space between frenzied movement and non-movement."

His work also develops through his experiments with dance therapy in several psychiatric hospitals. This openness toward mankind is an essential part of his artistic vocation.

Min Tanaka

Naked, his athletic body alive with flashes and starts, he crumbles to the ground, rolls gently onto his side or obsessively repeats the same gesture. Raw art, we are tempted to say. His dance provokes a profoundly primitive atmosphere that gives him an aura of mystery.

Min Tanaka began his career as a professional basketball player. Dissatisfied with sports, he turned to modern dance, which he studied for eight years. "To practice a sport is to experience limitations: you cannot go beyond the body. It was to overcome such limitations that I became a dancer."

Aware that what he was learning was unfulfilling, he decided to rediscover dance on his own and for himself. In order to accomplish this he used the naked body and immobility as his basis, trying to re-invent movement.

In his first performances—the "Subject" series (1973–1975), the "Butoh" series (1975–1977), the "Drive" hyperdance series (1977–1981)—his objective was to express the subconscious of his muscles, the memory of his cells. "It is like a sort of emotion which we are unable to understand, yet which moves us." During this period his movements appeared totally involuntary; his body moved by itself, slowly, like an amoeba. His dancing resembled undulating algae, caught in the current, or a cloud floating across the sky. It was the zero degree of dance, the very pulse of life.

Since the series called "Emotion" (1982–1986), he has tried more and more to integrate elements of daily life into his work. "That is why I now use costumes like sportswear or a raincoat, or props such as logs, a shovel, or a pail of water, as well as my voice—all of these things are part of the experience of daily life."

Little by little his dance has grown more "conscious"; whereas all gestures previously stemmed from the body's inner vibrations, he now allows for voluntary, even rhythmic movements.

Above and beyond his work as a solo performer, Min Tanaka tries to share his theories and his passion for dance off the stage as well as on. He conducts dance therapy sessions in centers for the handicapped, as well as organizing numerous workshops abroad each year. Dancers are also invited to his "Body Weather Laboratory" near Tōkyō, where the semi-communal lifestyle reflects and nourishes the artistic experience. Working outside the dance world remains essential for Min Tanaka. He works constantly with all kinds of musicians and visual artists in an ongoing endeavor to renew his dance. It is with this conviction that he is also the main force behind Plan B, an "alternative performance space" in Tōkyō where all types of artists, both Japanese and foreign, are invited to present their work. He is also the organizer of the Hakushu Festival, held every summer in the mountains near Tokyo, where performing and visual arts are offered in an open-air setting.

In 1981, he formed the group Mai-juku, composed of young dancers who had trained in his laboratory. Since then he has increasingly dedicated himself to this group whose performances manage to convey the pioneer spirit of butoh without falling back on imagery. Symbols of the modern age are freely played with: bicycles, work tools, or reams of paper, as opposed to nostalgic images of traditional Japan such as the kimono or the *shamisen*.
Recently, Min Tanaka has been concentrating on bigger dramatic productions that he develops over several months as work in progress. In these productions, his dance evokes the primordial emotions and feelings of human beings relating directly to nature.

"I don't dance in the place, but I am the place." M. Tanaka

"Our bodies love tradition; I feel butoh when I face my traditional body . . . Avant-garde is in an intense love affair with tradition."
M. Tanaka

"When I improvise, there is a certain design. It is like a phase on a path of a dream." M. Tanaka

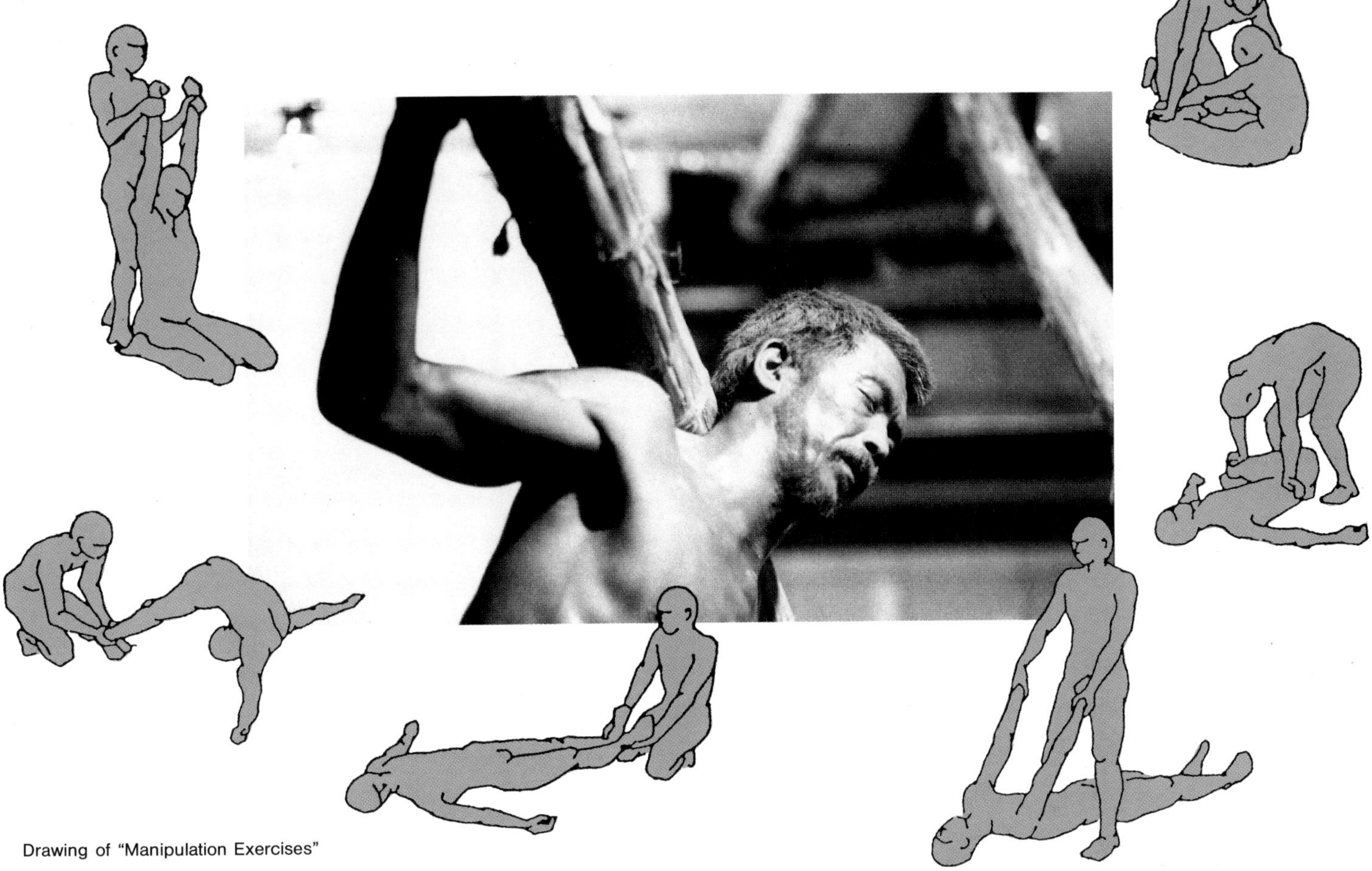

Drawing of "Manipulation Exercises"

Teru Goi

Teru Goi was trained in modern dance before coming under the influence of the work of Hijikata. Although he did not actually study butoh, his work came closer and closer to it.

His sets are generally piles of junk objects (old *tatami*, broken bicycles, bamboo curtains, poultry cages), and his solos represent the violence of an outcast of society, constantly flinging himself against the walls behind which life has imprisoned him.

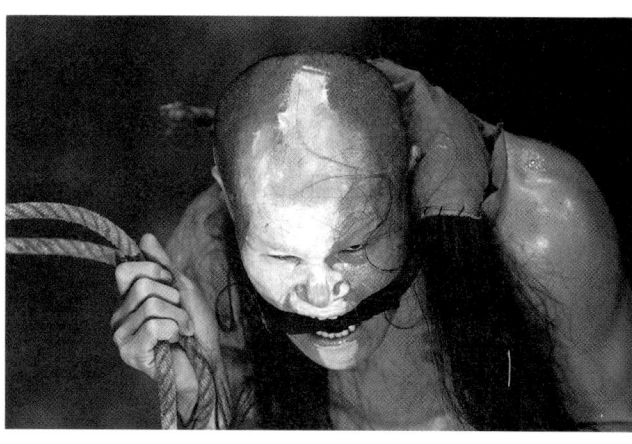

The New Generation of Butoh

With the appearance of a number of young dancers, we are witness to the birth of a "new generation" of butoh. The new butoh dancer works alone—his solitude is itself a response to the intellectual torpidness of Japan in the eighties. All taste for the spectacular quality and the provocativeness of Ankoku Butoh has been set aside. Now the dance itself is the focal point, experienced as an intimate adventure. For the dancer, this is not an easy path, for any sense of theatricality has been rejected. What results is an extremely aesthetic butoh, devoid of violence, directed towards purely physical experiences.

These soloists live in a world in which butoh is an accepted art form; they did not have to struggle to establish this new concept of dance, but rather adopted it as their own. Their work, while sometimes very sophisticated, often lacks the creative vigor which nourished the work of their masters. Their performances are sometimes chaotic and interminable, and seem to lack structure or even any real substance. What generally remains is the inanity of an aesthetic statement without any authentic backing.

Amongst all of these dancers, swept along by the ever-growing wave of the "butoh phenomenon," a few incontestably original and authentic artists stand out. Most of these are students of Kazuo Ōno or Akira Kasai, a few are self-taught.

While Ōno's art seems to flower in countless dimensions—a great variety of styles and techniques are visible in his work—none of his students has been able, or has even tried to absorb them all. Each has, however, developed a specific aspect of Ōno's work.

The work of Minoru Hideshima reflects the "mime" technique found in his teacher's dancing. His gestural quality helps sculpt a character, and his dance is often very concrete, directly linked to daily life. When he performs he seems like a melancholic Pierrot trapped in an absurd world, creating a universe reminiscent of that of Samuel Beckett.

Mitsuyo Uesugi worked, for a long time, as a model for painters and sculptors. While posing, she began to explore the notion of presence. She expresses the weight of life, the density of being—but always in relationship to an ideal, statue-like body.

Kunishi Kamirio, Hiroko Horiuchi, and Setsuko Yamada stand out from the ranks of Tenshi-kan. As Akira Kasai had done, Kunishi Kamirio gathered many young dancers around him at his school, Saraham-kan. His dance studio has become a meeting place for former Tenshi-kan members who, like his own students, give performances there.

His own performances, often inspired by Shintō culture, recall the religious, yet grotesque universe of *kagura*.

Both Hiroko Horiuchi and Setsuko Yamada have given up the mystique so essential to their teacher. In their delicate solos, they abandon their bodies to the whims of their imagination, in what appear as long dream sequences interspersed with tempestuous and erotic images.

Dance Green People

Mitsuyo Uesugi

"It is our nightmare or an obscene dream that visits a girl's slumber with fictitious innocence, a future-telling dream that a wizard peeps into." M. Uesugi

Masaki Iwana was initially an actor, but turned to dance after seeing Akira Kasai perform. He refused to take classes, however, preferring to develop his own technique based on his practice of yoga. Naked, he lets himself be carried by the space, and rid of all consciousness, abandons himself to those impulses which the environment provides. His work, totally unspectacular, represents the experience of the limits of the origins of dance. In his most recent works he tried to be more theatrical and to incorporate elements from everyday life in his dance.

We should also mention one of Mr. Ōno's earliest students, Moritsuna Nakamura who has created the "Dance Green People" group with Minoru Hideshima. Isso Miura, Tetsurō Fukuhara, Nada Natsugiwa, Daisuke Yoshimoto, Yasuko Takeuchi, and Takuya Ishide also deserve to be mentioned. Butoh has attracted a lot of followers, and it would be impossible to name all these solo dancers. The line between professionals and amateurs is not very clear, because there is no formal butoh school, no precise butoh technique. Many people who call themselves butoh dancers are motivated not so much by any particular talent for dance as by a desire to rebel against society. They have joined the butoh movement because they feel more comfortable there; for them, butoh has become a refuge from conventional society.

"It is just as if we had been playing together until we were fifteen years old.... So when we dance, we try to remember these forgotten games." M. Hideshima

Setsuko Yamada

Butoh in the rice field, event with Moritsuna Nakamura and several butoh members.

"My methodology then—naked, silent, standing still—was a manifestation of my desire to avoid being fenced in by the meaning of the language. It was an effort to approach substance, a yearning for language in its deepest sense of the word." Masaki Iwana

Kunishi Kamirio

Nada Natsugiwa

Daisuke Yoshimoto

On the Fringe of Butoh

There are a number of artists on the fringes of butoh, from where they have found the inspiration and the energy for their work without becoming part of the movement itself.

Among these, special mention must be made of Giriaku, a self-proclaimed street performer, a vagabond creator who works in parks and public places. His dance is very extroverted, reminding us of a clown, while at the same time it is as carefully controlled as mime. One of his most impressive pieces is based on the theme of a blind *shamisen* player, and ends in a disarticulated trance and a parody of "Swan Lake."

Shirō Daimon is another such figure. His background was in *Nihon buyō* and *kabuki* before he began his dance-happenings, often accompanied by jazz. Despite the fact his work has not yet reached maturity, an appreciably strong personality does appear in his dancing.

Butoh has also inspired numerous stage directors, in particular Shuji Terayama and Kara Jūro, two of the instigators of the non-institutional theater movement known as "Shōgekijō-undō" (little-theater movement). Of the younger directors, Shogo Ōta, the director of the group Tenkei Gekijō, deserves special mention. His emphasis on silence, slow motion and the expression of his characters' inner world makes his performances a kind of choreography of daily life. A good example of this is his totally silent piece, "Mizu no eki" (The Watering Hole). But he diverges from butoh in his faithfulness to a linear narrative structure which brings his work unquestionably closer to the world of theater.

Giriaku

CHAPTER V
EVOLUTIONARY CHANGES

In its twenty-five years of existence, butoh's development has been impressive. One cannot help but be surprised by its evolution: from the first "performance-happenings" of the early sixties to today's slick, professional productions.

This evolution goes hand in hand with a great diversification of technique, creating a number of currents, as seen in the preceding chapters. Each of these currents, however, has endeavored in its own manner to express the gestural universe, the cultural force, of the Japanese body.

This form of dance, which originated at the fringes, is now increasingly being recognized in Europe, the United States, and most recently in Japan itself, where media coverage denied hitherto, has finally brought it into the public eye. Although the majority of the population, even in intellectual and artistic circles, continues to reject this movement—which presents an image of society difficult to accept—it can no longer be ignored.

Yet paradoxically, the very success of butoh has been detrimental to it. Originally an expression of revolt, it has become the expression of a narcissistic need to please. Because too many concessions are being made to the audience, its force and authenticity have given way to aesthetic considerations. Over-confidence has dulled the sense of self-criticism which would have helped it to develop and be renewed.

The systematic rejection of meaning and discourse leaves butoh rather self-obsessed, and makes way for unerring repetition of its own impotence of expression.

Only by opening itself towards the world and mankind, only by exploring the society of which it is a part, is butoh likely to escape the dead end of both Ankoku Butoh's academicism and the weak aestheticism of the new generation of dancers.

Butoh has reached adulthood: is it capable of confronting maturity courageously without becoming enmeshed in sterile self-satisfaction, without becoming weighed down by a rhetoric of rejection in which it no longer even believes?

Certain groups are already trying to shake off the facile Japanese costumes and sets, retaining only the dance work itself. They are exploring new themes, looking to Eastern culture in general, leaning toward theatricalization, and developing its more pictorial or purely grotesque aspects.

Does the future of butoh reside in its involvement with the different tendencies in modern dance abroad? Many groups are already established in Europe and in America (Sankai-juku, Ariadone and Sebi in Paris; Poppo Shiraishi, Eiko and Koma in New York) where they are exposed to Western culture. At the same time, Western groups are beginning to be inspired by butoh in their own work (for example Studio D, L'Esquisse, and Maguy Marin in France). Perhaps this exchange heralds the opening of new paths and new hopes for dance in general.

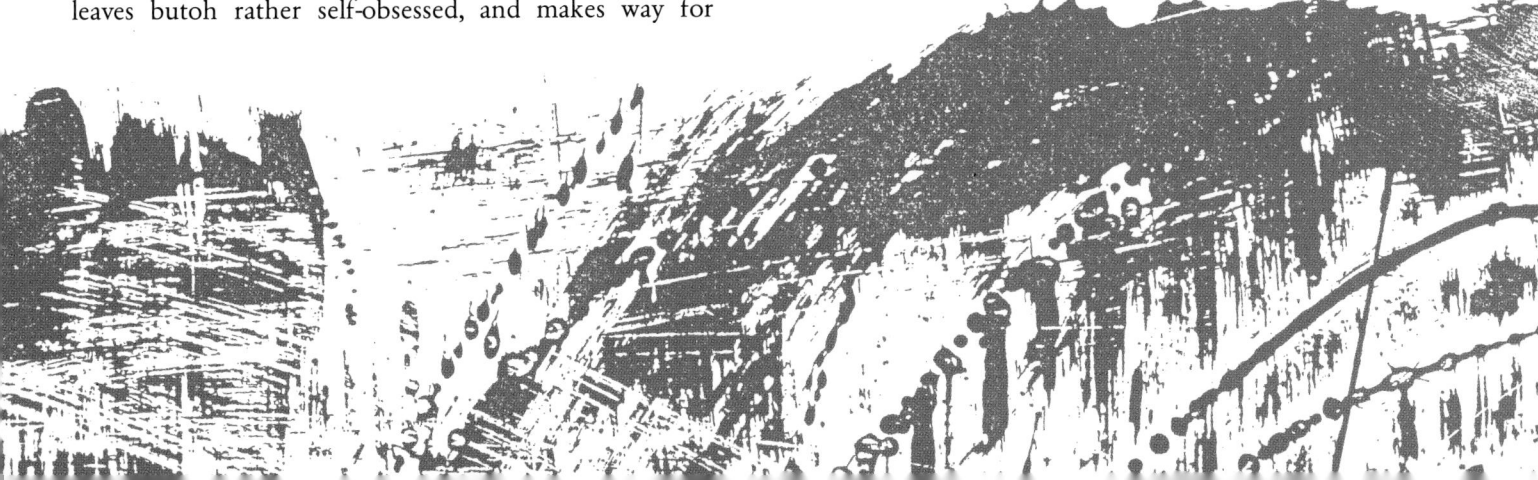

Monthly programs of Plan B

M. Ishii's pamphlet, "O Genet," 1967

M. Ishii's pamphlet, "Jizai," 1987

M. Tanaka's news letter, 1980

Dance Green People's pamphlet, 1987

Butoh performance directed by T. Hijikata with Y. Ashikawa, N. Nakajima, Reisen Lee, S. Yotsuya, etc., "Bicycle Race," 1967

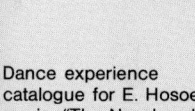

Dance experience catalogue for E. Hosoe movie, "The Navel and the Bomb," 1960

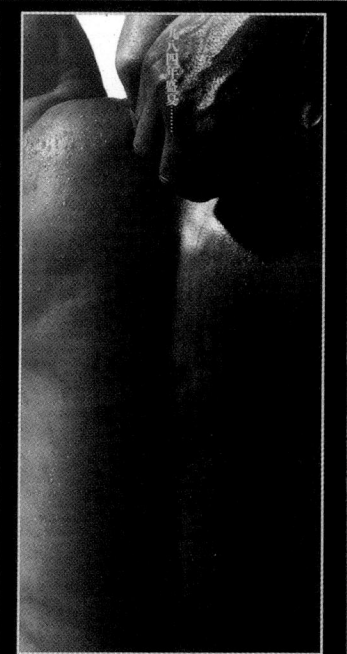
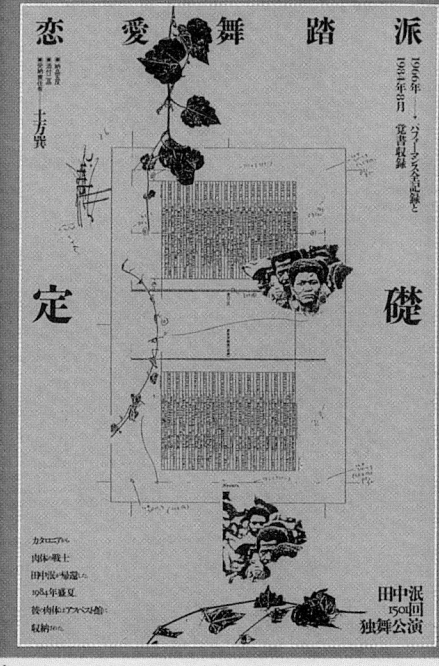

M. Tanaka's retrospective catalogue, 1984

APPENDIX

NOTES ON BUTOH

NOTES BY KAZUO ŌNO

What is a lesson?

In order to dance, I always wonder where to begin. When we think about human life in general, two points of view are possible. On the one hand we have humanism, based on profound love or idealistic feelings; on the other hand, pragmatism, which is directly linked to basic human needs or desires.

I think our lives are based upon these two ways of looking at life. And I don't think that dance can be seen independently from the notion that man lives. This may seem evident, but where do we begin to dance? At this point, I always hesitate. Were I to begin dancing without asking that question, I would be neglecting human life. I feel that dance must grow out of the gravity of human life, out of the confusion of life itself.

Dance begins with daily gestures. When someone comes to me wishing to dance, I always tell him that it will take at least five years. During those five years, I teach him to analyze and organize his own body gestures, while deepening his consciousness of life. Throughout the learning process it is essential that neither of these directions be neglected and that the body itself be situated at the heart of the dilemma.

During these lessons, a number of questions come up concerning wisdom in everyday life, self-respect and respect for others, the understanding of nature. Certain other themes are essential: the joy and pain of living, the wounds which life has dealt us or others, the gifts and ravages of nature.

Our bodily wounds eventually close and heal. But there are always hidden wounds, those of the heart, and if you know how to accept and endure them, you will discover the pain and joy which is impossible to express with words. You will reach the realm of poetry which only the body can express.

There is a certain area which can be taught in dance and a limit beyond which it is impossible to go. For example—let us suppose one wants to give a class on the theme "a Prayer to the Lord." Through your body you would have to express everything that the theme involves, and I would understand your slightest gesture. The problem is that for me, to dance in such a way that the images which portray a given theme are comprehensible is only the preliminary step. The true problem is elsewhere. What is really important is how you are going to deal with all the thoughts about life which this theme evokes, and then how you are going to approach the serious reality of life itself.

At this point, I have nothing more to teach you; you alone know the way. And dancing should give you the possibility to deal consciously with this serious reality of life.

I mentioned that I tell my students it takes five years to learn to dance. During the first few years, they study elementary movement and they try to become aware of their behavior in daily living. But the area which I cannot teach, which words cannot describe, must already exist.

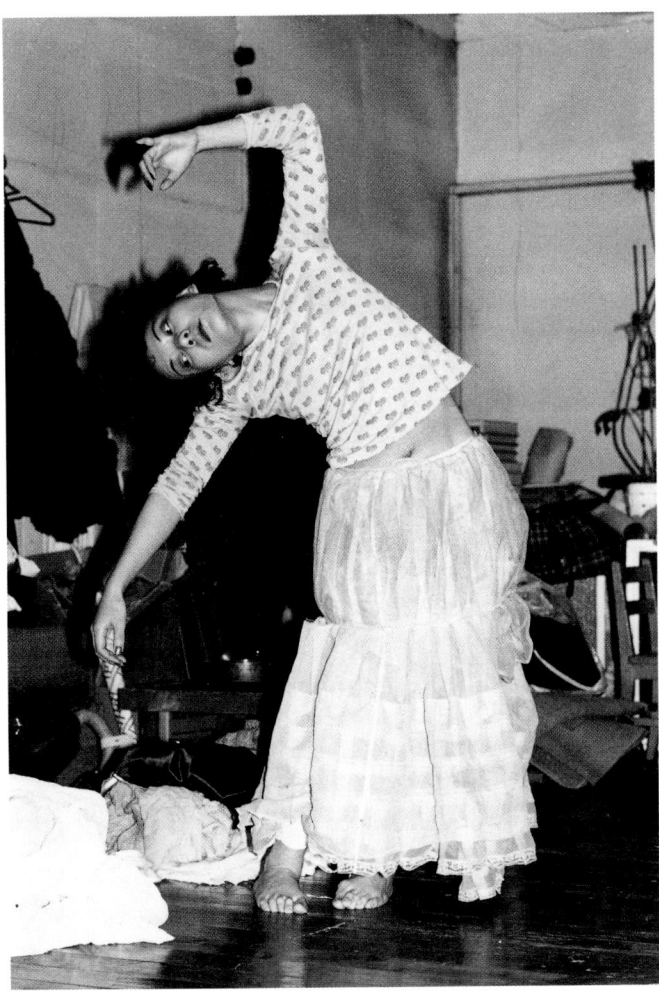
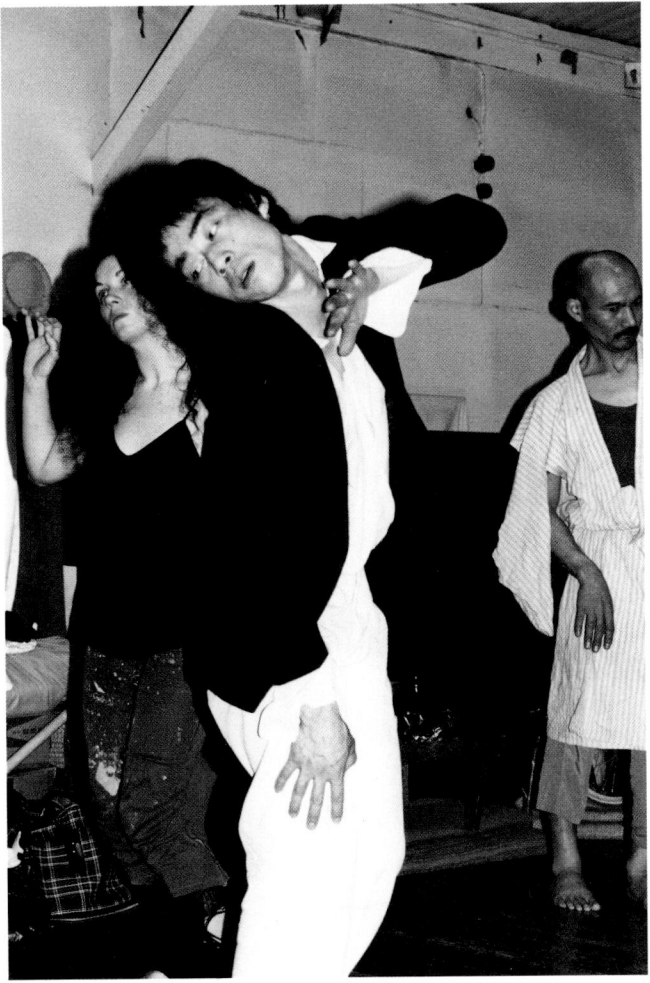

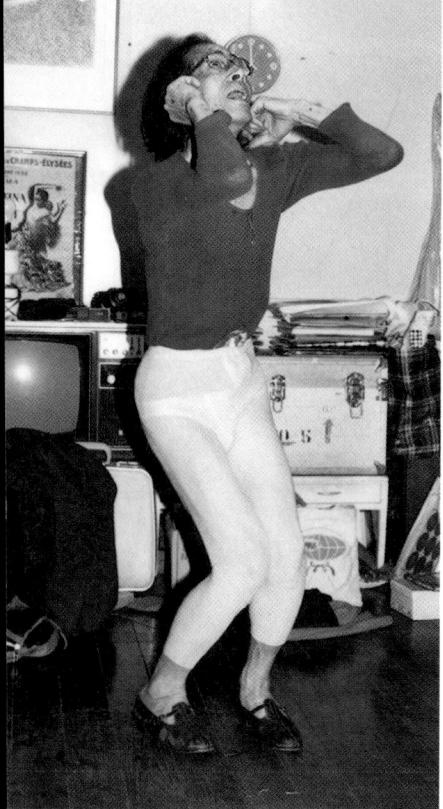

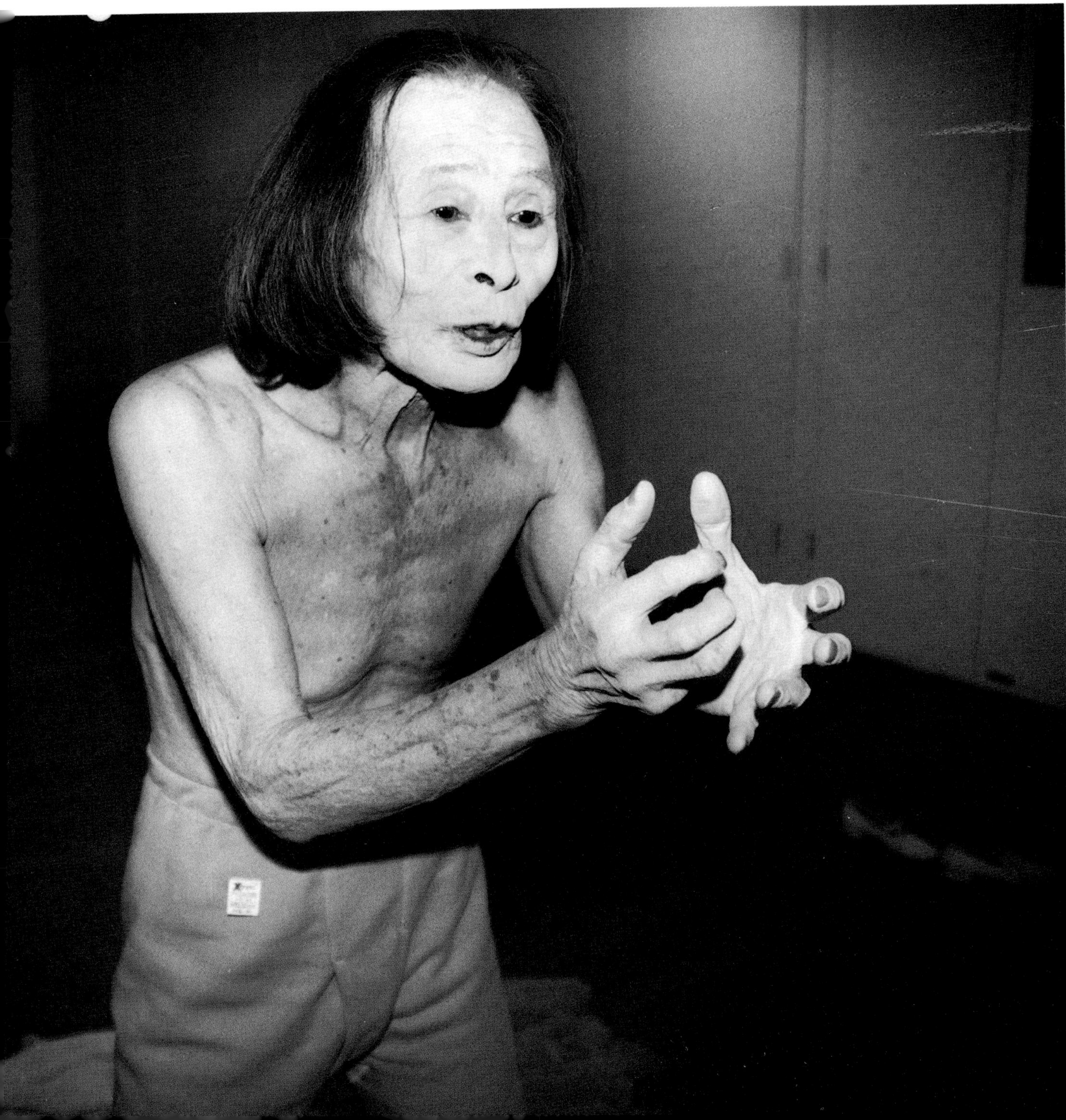

My Encounter with La Argentina

More than fifty years ago, while a gymnastic student, I saw La Argentina dance for the first time. I was invited along to see the Spanish dancer perform by a friend of mine, Yoshio Monden.

Seeing her dance is something I could never forget. We had seats at the rear of the third floor of the Imperial Theater. From the very first sight of her, I was spellbound; I was totally bewitched by her charm. It was truly an unforgettable encounter.

Some fifty years have passed in the meantime and during these years, I have experienced much regarding living and dancing. I have had flashbacks of La Argentina throughout these years. Her memory has lived with me in the depths of my soul, although I was never to witness her intense presence again before my eyes, no matter how I longed to see her.

Then, in 1976, I had the occasion to visit a one-man show by the painter Natsuyuki Nakanishi. I was about to leave the exhibition when I was struck by a painting near the exit. It was an oil painting of geometrical curves painted on a zinc sheet. I cried to myself "Aah, Argentina... it's you!"

Nakanishi-san had never had the opportunity to meet Argentina and, moreover, knew nothing about her life. He unwittingly had painted the spirit of Argentina; I could feel her presence, I could see her there among the flowing curves.

This unexpected encounter with Argentina led me to return to dancing on stage in order to express my profound admiration for her. While I stood there under the spell of the painting, I felt her come to life again. I realized that even after my ashes had been put in the urn, I would continue to seek her.

On returning home in this excited state I had yet another surprise awaiting me. On my desk lay some material on Argentina sent to me by one of my students in New York.

A photograph of her appeared in one of the programs... she smiled at me and whispered: "Shall we dance?" She asked me gently, cheering me up no end while I kept nodding. "Shall we dance, Ōno-san... dance with me."

Through the medium of this one painting and this one photograph I was able to meet up with her again; all my warm feelings for her were evoked and poured into a dance performance in her honor in November 1977.

The following year during May and June I performed this piece, called "Admiring La Argentina," at several venues in Europe. In Nancy, I was informed indirectly by a member of the audience of the existence of La Argentina's grave in the suburbs of Paris. Alas, I didn't meet this person; it is a great regret to me as I would like to thank whoever it was from the bottom of my heart. Miracles succeeded each other. Before my departure for Paris, I received a book titled "Argentina"; I was in seventh heaven over this incident. I cried for joy, "It's a miracle."

On arriving in Paris I immediately went to her grave in Neuilly. It was as if I were visiting my bride... In the book which I received, there was a photograph of La Argentina clad in a fur coat standing in a wasteland; it reminded me of her tragic death. It is a heavy burden to live. That noble and most beautiful being, La Argentina, had to perish, although she must have longed for eternity. I was afflicted by these painful thoughts while standing by her grave.. the price she paid to live... it was so heartbreaking. I clung to her gravestone not wanting to leave her... ever.

The third miracle was such a beautiful one. On the first day of our performance in Paris I danced to a piece composed by da Falla, to which Argentina had also danced. Among the audience were a niece and nephew of La Argentina accompanied by their families.

The following day I was invited to their home and was presented with a book containing photographs, Argentina's personal correspondence, autographs and paraphernalia.

On visiting her nephew's home, I was shown slides of her, accompanied by a tape of the castanets that she used to play. This one-hour-and-ten-minute show was so overwhelming that words do not suffice to express the awe and excitement I felt.

All these wonderful experiences, which are like miracles to me—visiting her grave, meeting her next of kin and receiving fragments of her life—left me with a great sense of indebtedness for being able to come close to her again. I returned to Japan with a handful of earth from her grave and a photodocumentary of her life.

Drawing by Nourit M.S.

"I had read about the creation of the world in the Bible; I'd always accepted it as a legend, but in La Argentina's work I saw it realized in front of my eyes. If this is creation I would like to lift one corner of it."

After returning home to Japan, I slowly eased back into my routine life. I listened to La Argentina's tape of "Granada" played on her castanets. The time I spent with her while listening to the beautiful sound of her castanets is truly precious to me . . . at such times I'm compelled to believe in eternal life.

It remains for me to thank all of those who made it possible for me to come into contact with a great source of joy and inspiration in my life, the beautiful Argentina . . . .

The Dead Sea (manuscript notes)

The mountains which surround the Dead Sea were formed out of salt. I thought that nothing could live there and was surprised to see small rodents scurrying between the rocks. It was as though these animals, who seemed to feed on the very mountain itself, were being raised as its own children. And I suddenly felt very close to the animals; I, who taking form in my mother's womb, had fed on her life. I will never forget these creatures, upright on their hind legs, crying out that the mountain belonged to them.

The fetus experiences the whole flow of time from the creation of the world—from the very first cell to the man of today. When he touches one hand with the other, it is an important experience for him. He has touched his own hand, but also the hand of his mother, and without knowing it, the hand of the cosmos.

Life engenders the cosmos, the cosmos engenders life. They are but one. In this way, the child is not only conscious of his state of becoming, but also of his state of being a child. Likewise, the fetus is conscious of existing as a fetus.

The mother's womb is small, but for the fetus it is as large as the cosmos, unbelievably large. It is like paradise;

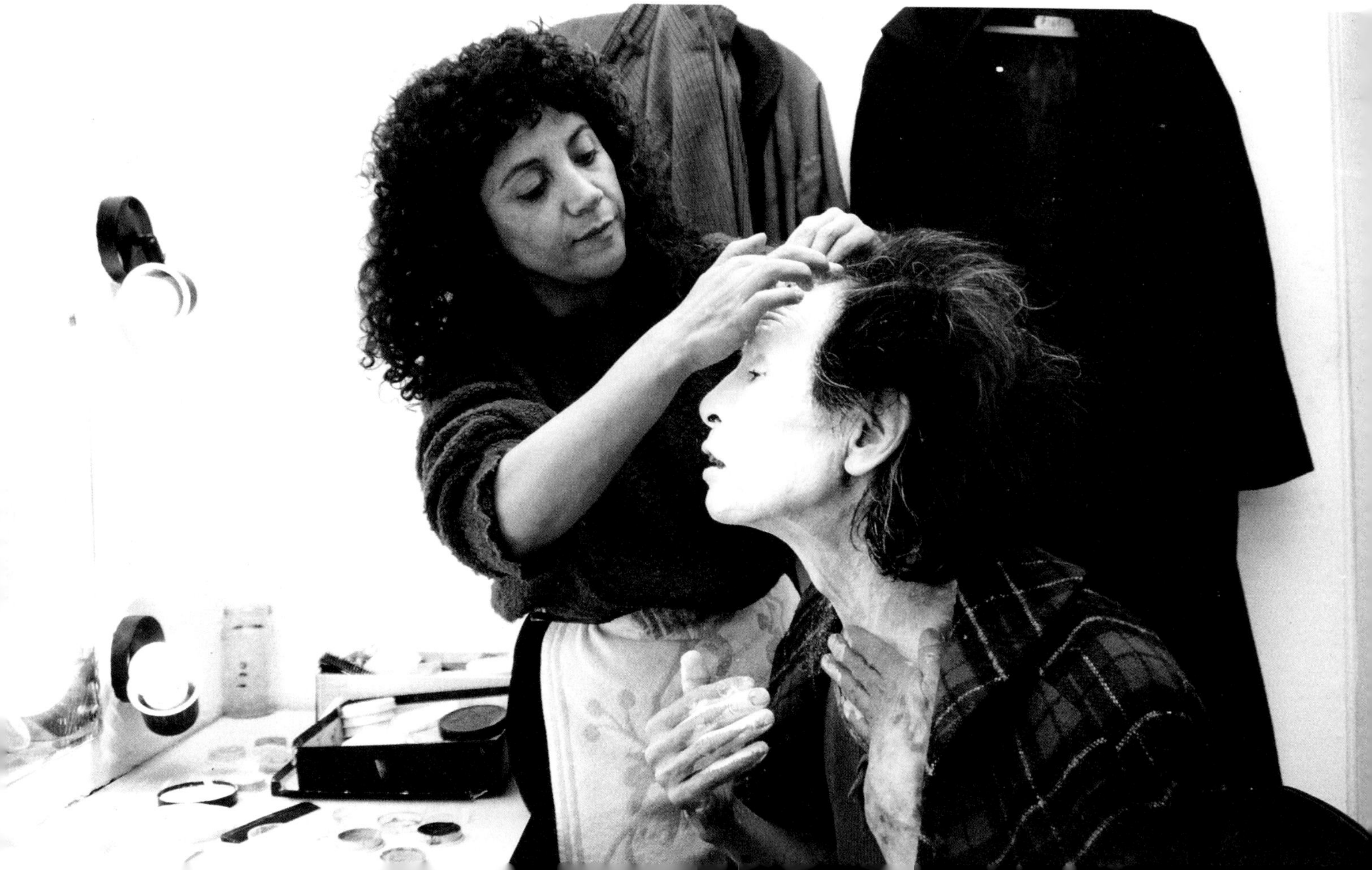

Drawing by Nourit M.S.

having nothing, it has everything....

When I first arrived in Israel in 1983, standing on the heights surrounding the Dead Sea, I felt projected into ancient times.

Before the shifting of certain tectonic plates, this sea was once connected to the Mediterranean Sea. But the junctions were blocked, and after a period of torrid heat, it became the Dead Sea. The shifting of the plates still continues, at a rhythm marked by billions of years.

As I looked around, I felt I was in a tiny corner of this history, the day after the creation of the world.

All the energy of the cosmos seemed concentrated in these animals, running freely across the mountainside. As they watched me, their calls resounded in my heart, a choir celebrating the creation of the world.

This long transformation, taking place over billions of years, is it not because a ghost was trapped or forgotten, that the tectonic plates continue to shift? On these mountains where no grass grows, searching for my thoughts in all the suffering, I myself become a ghost, I take his form, and stretch out my hand to reach him.

It doesn't matter what ghost: what matters is to meet him.

A living ghost.

A dead ghost.

A ghost pursuing death throughout eternity.

While I was in a nook in the mountains, I felt that the tectonic plates were beginning to move within me. There I was in the land of Israel, which had experienced the tectonic upheavals, and I began to hear the mass which comes from nowhere, and resounds in suffering since the beginning of time. Today, the tectonic plates continue their dance, and I keep the echo of that mass in my heart.

For my performance, I would like to begin by that mass. Concentrating all of the energy of the ghost and of the Viennese waltz within me, I would like to dance aided by the strength of the animals from the Dead Sea.

Morning Greetings

The scenario is the pond of Monet's garden in Giverney, the water lilies in bloom. Monet's final works focus on the reality and transparency motif beginning from the surface of the pond's expanse.

I was walking by the garden pond when we ran across each other and after exchanging morning greetings I wanted to show him my complete autobiography (or possibly that of everybody) depicting among other works my dance of the good morning dream at Giverney.

Did I create this piece or did this piece create me?

When I look at this composition, I'm unsure of its origin. I have to calm my pounding heart.

The figure of a woman stretches along Halley's comet, wandering eternally in the cosmos. It must be Mary who seems to be touching the limits of the universe.

The ship which carries the disorder of the dead continues just as the dead carry love.

Ave Maria. Her tears have dried, her arms are powerless. These are the arms which move like death, earnestly imploring the figure of Jesus.

Superimposition of the world of reality and the surreal world.

Aren't the void and the reality one and the same? And couldn't Halley's comet be Joseph, the husband of Mary?

NOTES BY TATSUMI HIJIKATA

Interview

Butoh has the best capacity for expression in the world... Take, as an example, the *shosagoto* dance plays where everyday movements and gestures are incorporated into butoh, or even into the *kabuki* or *nō* for that matter. This phenomenon is unique to Japan. This is because the Japanese have a fundamentally anarchic concept of the body. When we walk our feet slip to one side and we are continually off balance. There are no paths to follow and even the sky poses a threat; consequently our way of walking is so unsure... for me there were only the borders of the paddy fields to help me find my way. The same can be said of our colors that are those of grilled rice cakes on a festive occasion.

Our concept of the body is truly anarchic. The poet Sakutarō Hagiwara wrote "Beneath the hat, there is a face." The fact that there is a face beneath the hat is obvious, yet the Japanese still find it strange. We immediately feel that the body is bound up with something strange.

It is said of the body that many of the rhythms and steps of Japanese folkloric dances were introduced to the peasants by a visiting monk from Tōkyō in return for his board and lodging. This was to help and encourage them in their work.

I'm convinced that a pre-made dance, a dance made to be shown, is of no interest. The dance should be caressed and fondled; here I'm not talking about a humorous dance but rather an absurd dance. It must be absurd. It is a mirror which thaws fear. The dancer should dance in this spirit....

In other forms of dance, such as flamenco or classical dance, the movements are derived from a fixed technique; they are imposed from the outside and are conventional in form. In my case, it's the contrary; my dance is far removed from conventions and techniques... it is the unveiling of my inner life.

For example, take these fingers. They are capable of catching objects. But I've asked myself in an extreme situation what their function could be between one articulation and another. There are things which are not apparent in our daily lives. This is exactly what I want to show—those aspects of our lives which are not apparent to us.

But, if in fact one were to remove from their dance both the hardship and the cruelty they endured, very little would remain. The origins of Japanese dance are to be found in this very cruel life that the peasants endured. I have always danced in a manner where I grope within myself for the roots of suffering by tearing at the superficial harmony.

We must confront our bodies: thinking about the strangeness of our bodies or manipulating them through various training techniques is not enough.

I dislike the idea, let alone the creation of a "regular" dance or theater troupe... I'm not in search of such superficiality between people. I prefer to go deep inside the person, to lose myself in this body so as to meet with him body and soul. I could, for example, make him unmask himself by telling him "Your eyes are ghastly, you, who have always lived just like everybody else, and this is because you have always been so alienated from your own flesh and blood."

In the Stanislavski system or in the techniques of other national dances, it is to a certain degree that such and such an effect can be produced, that the articulation can be categorized... thus man finds himself in a narrow and constricted world.

Since we all have blood flowing through our veins, the observation of our body always finishes by being obscure... we are not transparent. Criminal, the body has something in common with the criminal. This is not a theoretical point; it's the practical dimension in man's life, his animal instincts, his primal nature.

One finds this in the dance of the Gypsies; their life is not easy, moreover they steal in order to live. They are a free people and their dances are correspondingly intense in their purity. The origins of Spanish dance are to be found in the dance of the Gypsies.

It is possible to make a superb dance with the eyes alone. Everybody has the inherent ability to dance. When students come to take a course, the first thing I ask them is "What has brought you here?"...

I carry the theater round with me; the building itself is part of the dance, even the ticket. Thus, when the audience returns home, they carry part of the dance with them. Everything is interlocked: the dance, the building, the theater. It is just a different way of viewing the structure of the theater.

Imagine that a spectator at the cinema masturbates; he goes contentedly to the cinema. His sense of well-being is derived firstly from the darkness, and then from being seated alone in his solitude. This has been known to happen in the Musashino-kan. Rats scurry about while one watches the movie... at this moment the French actress who appears on the screen lets out a scream as she begins to set herself aflame. The copy is of poor quality and already the spectators have begun to cry out "We want our money back." When the showing is over, he goes to the toilets and there a satyr awaits him... it's natural. To me, that's all part of the show.

Man, once dead, crawl back!

Anxiety has sown itself everywhere. It lies always ahead of the action, just like the school kid who pisses in his pants just as the whistle blows at the school races.

This form of anxiety is growing—anxiety over the present, anxiety over the future. However, there is not the slightest trace of fear in this condition. I wonder how it can be that this situation arose.

There is a lot of anxiety present at my dance lessons: one finds there many people festering due to their own turbid eroticism. All kinds gather at the studio, some forlorn, some just passing through. In teaching butoh my aim is to make them aware of a part of themselves that they have lost contact with, by making them study themselves body and soul. They are inhibited by their anxieties, but through

the means of dance they can share their anxieties with each other.

Learning dance is not a matter of where to position an arm or a leg. Since I believe neither in a dance teaching method nor in controlling movement, I do not teach in this manner. I have never believed in these systems; I have been mistrustful of them since the day I was born.

Recently, it is possible to distinguish between the fighters and the pleasure seekers in this life. On the one hand, those who throw bombs, and on the other hand, those who are completely indifferent. Superficially they

seem to be at extremes, but they share one thing in common: their homogeneity. They are mistaken in thinking that hurling bombs or turning away makes them diametrically opposed. One should do both!

As an example, the troops that fight continually in battle tire quickly. If they were immersed in the spirit of butoh, one man would be able to do the work of two and recovery would be quicker. This butoh spirit is what I try to impart during lessons in my studio. Younger people start with great enthusiasm in some endeavor, but their ardor quickly cools off. This is because they are acquainted only with the superficial and ostentatious aspects of life. Through immersing oneself wholly in dance one can encounter the butoh spirit. It is here, rather than in the stage performance, that one finds the real meaning of butoh.

When one considers the body in relation to dance, it is then that one truly realizes what suffering is: it is a part of our lives. No matter how much we search for it from the outside there is no way we can find it without delving into ourselves.

We are broken from birth. We are only corpses standing in the shadow of life. Therefore, what is the point of

"Oh, I have not got the palms to pray for us who stand accused by a new born Butoh. So, I only stick out my tongue under the rain."

becoming a professional dancer? If a man becomes a laborer and a woman a servant, isn't that enough in itself!

That is the essence of butoh—and that is how I lead my communal life.

We should live in the present. We should do what we have to do now and not keep putting it on the long finger as the majority of adults do. This is why they exhaust themselves. For children, there is only the present. They are not afraid. Fear envelops us in a fine mesh. We must remove this mesh.

There is nothing to fear in the avant-garde; it's only a dry intellectual comprehension. We *should* be afraid! The reason that we suffer from anxiety is that we are unable to live with our fears. Anxiety is something created by adults. The dancer, through the butoh spirit, confronts the origins of his fears: a dance which crawls towards the bowel of the earth. I don't believe this is possible with European dance.

The body is fundamentally chaotic; the Japanese body particularly, which in comparison with the coherent body of the Occidental (both religiously and culturally), is unsure in its stance. Occidentals have their feet planted firmly on the ground, forming a pyramid, whereas the Japanese seem to be performing acrobatic feats on oil paper. Therefore, they have to find their balance on twisted legs.

For my next performance I plan to use *geta* (wooden sandals). There are now only seven artisans in Tōkyō capable of inserting the "teeth" for the foot strap. Eventually I will have to ask the craftsmen of the Osaka area. Gradually the environment in which we live is becoming a toothless one in every sense of the word.

Once fallen, man must rise again. It is not only a matter of straightening one's back and facing the sun. I am not interested in having an ordinary theater troupe, but rather a troupe which has experienced the vagaries of this world. Once, there was a very noticeable change in a member of the troupe who had returned after a period of absence. On being asked what had happened to him, he replied that he had been washing dishes! For these kind of people dance is a way of helping them from burning up; it acts as a lubricant. That is why I do not see any value in either literature or painting that does not contain the essence of butoh.

I abhor a world which is regulated from the cradle to the grave. I prefer the dark to the dazzling light. Darkness is the best symbol for light. There is no way that one can understand the nature of light if one never observes deeply the darkness. A proper understanding of both requires that both their inherent natures be truly understood.

One does not need to be dazzling like an alien from another star. I would like to construct a huge countryside in Tokyo.

The young should not become sensual addicts. They need a real desire and must act in accordance with it—

"Butoh can only be made by that which can be taken from the manner of living

dance with it, without imposing regulations on themselves.

Don't mince your steps, take a giant step!
One should believe in the energy born in oneself out of suffering.
One shouldn't become a *bonsai* (miniature tree).
Believe in your own energy and don't let yourself be affected by others.

Interview

Before the war, the only four commodities on the market in Tōkyō from the Tōhoku region were soldiers, geishas, rice, and horses.

At the beginning of spring, when the snow began to melt, I used to dive into the river. One day, I got sucked into a whirlpool which dragged me to the bottom of the river. My parents and the village people, thinking that I was either lost or had been kidnapped, searched for me high and low. I could hear their voices from the far end of the river. They finally found and rescued me.

Thus I was brought back to life; prior to this I had been saved from the uterine fluids and this time from the waters of the earth. And so too should the butoh dancer be perpetually reborn.

In Tōhoku, paddy fields are everywhere and the wind blows constantly. While the parents work afar in the rice terraces they leave their children in straw cradles. The child

cries but cannot be heard; his cries are stifled by the blowing wind while his parents continue their work unawares. It is thus that the baby learns through its body that his cries are unheard. He swallows his tears and nourishes himself on them, sobbing and hiccoughing; the child swallows the darkness. His body becomes his toy. At dusk, his parents come to remove him from the cradle, but his feet are tucked under him and he is unable to stand.

Western dance begins with its feet planted firmly on the ground whereas butoh begins with a dance wherein the dancer tries in vain to find his feet. What has happened to the tucked-in feet?

What has become of our bodies?

Straight legs are engendered by a world dominated by reason. Arched legs are born of a world which cannot be expressed in words.

of a people—gestures evolve from bodies which have been restrained for a long time within the traditional way of life."

NOTES BY NATSUYUKI NAKANISHI

The painter Natsuyuki Nakanishi has followed the butoh movement since its inception. He has designed sets and posters for Tatsumi Hijikata, Akira Kasai, and Sankai-juku among others. It was he who did the painting in which Ōno recognized La Argentina.

Working with Hijikata on a Poster

One night in an ill-lit couples bar in Meguro, Hijikata said to me "Nakanishi, Nakanishi, listen carefully to what I'm going to say: 'Thistle,' okay? 'thistle,' 'hunting dog,' 'the translator of the wind,' 'the first flower,' 'the burning dog's tooth,' 'saddle.' That's the cover for a horse's back. Okay? And also this, Nakanishi; it's not an edible image: 'an ordinary meal.' And '17 years.' When I say seventeen years, do you think I'm crazy? 'A stone thrown through the glass sign of a reanimation hospital.' Are you taking note of this? Also 'frog.'" When he asked me if frogs were toys to be dissected, I said "yes." Then he continued, "'tooth,' and 'Korean whistle,' 'sulphur,' 'worms,' 'laughter,' 'boiling,' 'the sphere of love.'"—The sphere of love? What's that? "It's a woman's womb. 'Korean volubis,' that's a poisonous plant," he said. "'Dreaming potion,' 'comb,' 'greenhouse,' 'shelled insect,' that's a ladybug." Then Hijikata added, "Make a poster with theses words."

Before creating his butoh dance, he asked me to note down his first images in the form of words. But as I listened, I didn't write anything. So I was able to transcribe the images directly onto the poster. One must dance from that principle, and a poster like that could never be concrete.

Pink Paint

This is what happened. Hijikata was performing a piece for which I hadn't designed the set. But he called me and said, "Nakanishi, I have a favor to ask you. Could you come over with that pink paint you always use?" When I asked him why, he said, "I'll give you a signal during my dance, and at that moment, pour the paint on my back." I was a bit embarrassed to get up in the middle of the audience and go on stage. I wondered how I would ever do it. Finally, I went with a painter who helps me in my studio, and I had him sit in front of me.

During the dance, Hijikata undid his belt and tossed it in our direction: that was the signal. I was to have gone up on stage, but instead I passed the paint to my assistant, who went and poured it on Hijikata's back.

When I thought about it later I realized that I had betrayed Hijikata. He wanted me to pour the paint. Not just anybody would do for the pink paint. If I had been as famous as Picasso, it would have been understandable. For the audience, I was nobody in particular, but for Hijikata, I was someone.

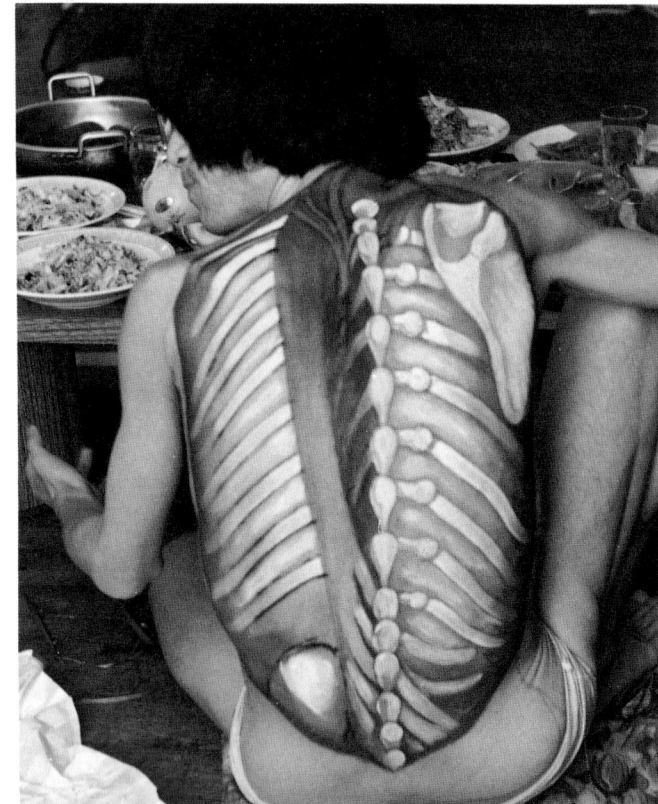

NOTES BY EIKŌ HOSOE

About *Kamaitachi*

Kamaitachi, or "Weasel's Sickles," when translated literally from the Japanese, is a record of the memory I experienced during World War II when I was evacuated from Tōkyō to the country village where my mother was born. I was twelve years old in 1944 when the American fire bombing was the worst. Most of the school children had to be evacuated to the remote countryside. Those who had no relatives were sent to the country to live communally. Those who had relatives in the country, as I did, were sent to live with them. Some had brothers or sisters, but my younger brother, then three years old, could not be separated from our mother and father who had jobs in Tōkyō.

I liked the landscapes and the environment of the country, but I hated the country itself. This feeling was due to the poor communication between the country boys and the neighborhood children. My relatives were very good to me, but when I would go out to the towns or villages, children playing around the corner watched me with old, cold eyes. It was hard for me to join them. It was not only me. Other children were from big cities like Tōkyō. We were called "city kids." They thought city kids were different from country kids. Farmers' children were plump, but we from the city were thin from hunger. Their laughing expressions were awful.

The dark, snowy country seemed to be full of ghosts. In fact, there were ghosts. We children were always frightened that something would catch us when we went outside after dark. Yuki-onna, or "Snow Woman," and Kamaitachi were among them. I pictured the Snow Woman not as terrible but, on the contrary, as rather romantic.

Kamaitachi, on the other hand, was something very awful. Kamaitachi is a small invisible animal which attacks good people walking in the rice field lanes in the late springtime. A man who is attacked by Kamaitachi finds his arms or legs or another part of his flesh sliced as if cut by a very sharp knife, but with no blood. In Japanese, *kama* means sickle, and *itachi* means weasel. So Kamaitachi is an invisible weasel, with very sharp teeth like a sickle. But no one has ever seen him. No one knows where or when he appears, only that he attacks people in the fields.

I had the strange feeling, though, that I should not hate the land where my mother was born. If I hated it, I would hate my own mother.

Kamaitachi, then, is a very personal record of my own memory from my boyhood, with all the complex feelings of love and hate from those days in the countryside.

Photography cannot directly express one's memory. But a photographer wants to record his memory. In writing? In painting? In singing? Photography? I wanted to express it in photography because I was a photographer. To do so I needed a catalyst. I found it in Tatsumi Hijikata, a good friend of mine and a great dancer. He was sympathetic to my ideas. Photography expresses the subjects themselves in their own time. Outwardly, this is a documentary of the dancer, Tatsumi Hijikata. At the same time, *Kamaitachi* is an inner document of myself and of my background in Japan.

NOTES BY KAZUKO SHIRAISHI

The Sorcerer of Butoh
(seventy years in the life of a fetus)

Maybe he's there crouched among the straw of some distant hayloft or then again among the wild reeds on the seacoast where the coarse sand grazes against the jaw.

   Somebody is squatting there.

   This squatting form releases itself into the world, drifting through the mists as if it were hovering between the Earth and Hades
   Approaching a breast
   Clinging to the breast of a large domestic beast, it could well be a sow
   Murmuring the sweet words of love
   Imploring it with caresses,

Maybe simply drinking
The sacred sperm
The milky liquid of desire
Longing in his heart
For the flesh, the form of some invisible spirit,
Murmuring whispers
As if waiting.

The fetus, on scrutiny
Reveals the unfurling saga of time on its skin,
   A witness to its premature entry into this world, be it that some seventy years have already passed,
   Sometimes one hears the rasping autumn wind cut through the silence like a flute just as one walks through a dead corpse.

Transforming into the eye of Hades
Its arrival pierces the shadows like a blinding light
The shadows begin to dance in the bowels of the earth
Maybe it's a specter or a phantom
Who could know at this stage?
It would bring with it the spirits of Hades to the surface of the earth and it would be known as the sorcerer of the shadows, this creature who drifts through the strange and marvelous landscape of Hades

Kazuo Ōno, Kazuo Ōno, Kazuo Ōno
Calling this name frequently like an incantation
Reveals the sorcerer like a bolt of lightening in the darkness
Announcing the birth of this strange fetus that has come from the kingdom of the deaf
And appeared in this world.

Maybe he's there crouched among the straw of some distant hayloft or then again among the wild reeds on the seacoast where the coarse sand grazes against the jaw.

Maybe on some farmhouse mat
One of those old tattered mats worn by the years
Where the spirits of the dead have reposed for thousands of years
Somebody is squatting there Praying
Eating
Eating with his fingers
A piece of his very own flesh
A very hardened piece of his own soul
Thinking that it will take possibly some millennia to swallow
Continuing to eat he begins to unwind slowly like a spool of wire thread, his body gradually unleashing itself into the world
Stretching and stretching
Expanding
Stretching
It finally vanishes
Leaping between
The depths of hell and paradise
Through Hades and the land of the living
Between the past and the future
Who knows where.

Even though this leap lasts a mere instant
It spans all of seventy years
The fetus

Butoh avidly devours the sun
Ending the putrifying gluttony
All butoh dancers have feet which rot while plodding along the earth,
Leaving only their arms
Which invoke a flabby dance gesticulating ecstatically
Oblivious to the fact that their form is unreflected in anybody's eye,
There were days when their arms limply danced incessantly
Propagating themselves
By dozens
By hundreds
By thousands
At that very moment
Deep in the earth
From the depths of the earth's womb
Is heard a cry
The primal scream, the natal cry
The fetus

Already a veteran
In the ways of the world
In each and every cell the wisdom and maturity of a seventy year life span
And in a flash of an eye
The experiences of his previous lives speak
His eyes shine and glare
Focusing steadily
At the core of Hades.

The future is known to these eyes
The eyes of the sacred prince of Hades
Leap over seventy years in an instant
The insolent flesh
Laden with experience
Bathed in the waters of time
Like a flame
Spewing forth on the present
The entrails of its past.

Maybe he's there crouched among the straw of some distant hayloft or then again among the wild reeds on the seacoast where the coarse sand grazes against the jaw.

Somebody is there
Somebody is there
Somebody
Is
There
Leaping in an instant
Towards eternity
Squatting
Is squatting.

Repose for a Soul in the Sky

I have never thought of such a death,
falling head first from the sky,
dying on the way to heaven.

Not a bird, but a man.
Not a god, but a human being.

He lived, committing no fault
against the beauty of existence,
with sincerity, with diligence,
for life's joy and ascension.

Fate struck him,
straight from the sky.
I ask you, God, where was your hand?
Be it your left or your right,
Was it not in your power to use it?
Straight from heaven into the sky,
Facing the fiery voice in the depths of the heart.

Oh, ascending spirit,
You who were so young!
So young, yet into the sky you fell.

—dedicated to Yoshiyuki Takada, dancer of Sankai-juku—

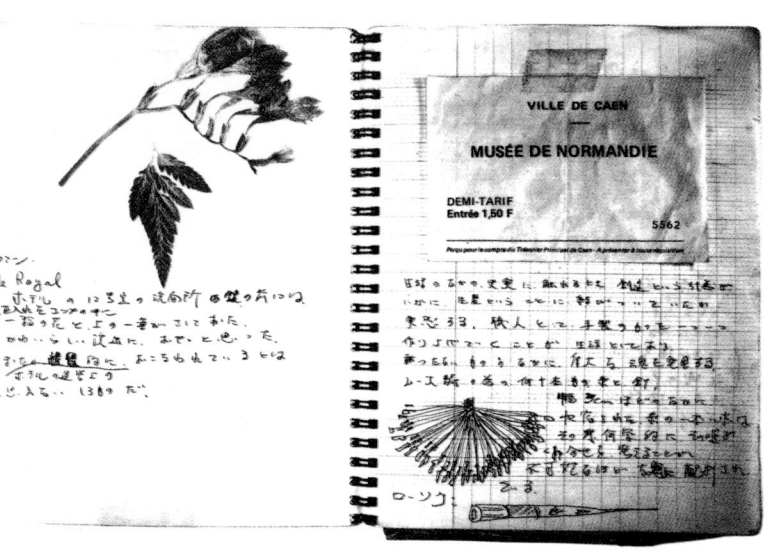

Sketches by Y. Takada from his notebook.

NOTES BY ISAMU ŌSUKA

The Tiger in the Bowels

The time when the stage had its mythical power has long since passed.

If happenings on the stage are to be not mere shadowgraphs of culture but real physical expressions in space, that is, creative processes in which the screams of all things in nature issue from them as momenta, the first thing we should do is to pull original scenes—from ancient times through the present—into our body, and to turn them into our own bowels. It is a search through the vast darkness of our body. When we set free the lonely tiger living in our body, we may arrive at our native place—our original scene. In order to fathom the mystery as to whence we have come, that is, to elucidate "the thing hung up" between what has happened and what will happen, we have to trace back the history of the body to remote antiquity—with whom did it associate and to what did it entrust itself? It will help bring the history of the body, which contains time and space, back to life on the stage, as well as lay personal history before the dusty audience. If the body is "nameless woods," the life of an insect such as a man depends entirely upon these woods. The spirits of our ancestors serve as catalysts, with which we can solve the mystery of the body. In other words, the body is an antenna, and the "thing," which has been kept in the body, will become visualized on the stage the moment it is hurled out of the body (as if out of a top spinning in space).

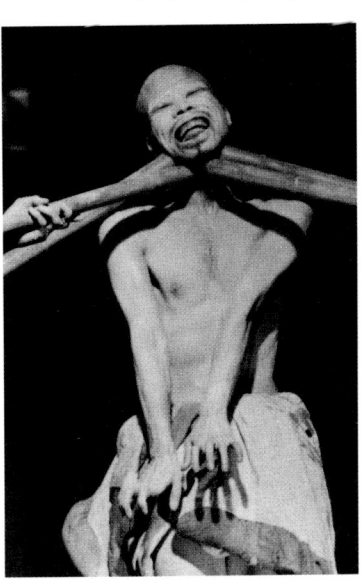

In order to catch alive the hunger of an original thing, the primitive reminiscence in the cells of the body, and a mythical archetype, we should organize all accidents. To dance on the stage is, after all, to produce a second nature there. We may say that the greater part of the activity of a dancer is to create the figure of his own bed as an elephant does its own grave.

NOTES BY USHIO AMAGATSU

The Distance Between Image and Dance

(Text for the program of "Jōmon-shō" by U. Amagatsu) When I think of dance, the image of a prehistoric painting comes to mind. I see the lines traced in the deepest, darkest part of a cave, as if to hide its existence, using non-linguistic representations. Dance can neither live within this painting, nor experience it.

To stand in the cave...

Deep in a part of the cave that could never be reproduced, it is filled with exquisite, unimaginable splits and fissures and rocky outbreaks, a succession of rich, eloquent images continues... ever-changing... to pass my vision.

To stand in the cave, to become the painter...

The painting emerges from intimate memories, closely linked to the experiences of living each day. It blooms on the wall with a vibrant, arresting reality—not simply a copy of the painter's world. It is the realization of images issuing from within the sensory realm, and directly linked with them.

To stand in the cave, to distance myself from the painting...

I emerge from behind the painter and am face-to-face with a fierce wild beast. I sense the distance between myself that hunts, and myself that watches the hunter. I discover myself seeing and hearing. When the form emerges I realize this relationship anew, and respond: moving from sight to watchfulness, from hearing to listening.

To depart from the cave...

(Text about "Kinkan Shōnen")

A performance has both beginning and end... common sense. But a circle, drawn by a compass, has starting and ending points, which disappear when the circle takes life.

The performance is a ceremony for the audience... their entry to the theater, seating... these are all part of the ceremony. The space itself participates... empty—full—empty... together with the performers. This is the state of a youth; he has a shaven head. I imagine him somewhere beside a sea... perhaps because I myself was born beside the sea. The boy dreams he is a fish... fragmented images like a collage.

The structure of Kinkan Shōnen is precise and exact, but there are always elements of improvisation, which alter the mood and interpretation of some sequences. The principal idea is deceptively simple... a dream of the origin of life, emergence from the sea, as the boy appears to stand on the shore and be drawn into the roar and echo of the life force. Within the cyclical nature of life are startling transformations and metamorphoses. The theme of the cycle runs throughout the performance, resurfacing in the penultimate scene... as the fish-men are caught, and flap helplessly on the shore. But the final scene goes beyond their capture, to a permanent blue stretching endlessly with unchanging expression.

NOTES BY AKAJI MARO

Sometimes I feel I can describe my body without my own body. First of all, you have to kill your body to construct a body as a larger fiction. And you can be free at that moment. It happens when you think about this concept that fiction equals a body. It is not only massive but also light and transparent. Therefore I wonder what does this fiction consist of . . . and I'm surprised how mysterious the body is. This fiction equals body is somehow really an Asian construction. When it opens its mouth, the dark cave in it belongs to something other than human beings.

This fiction is almost chaos. Catching some parts of chaos and creating a total chaos. Catching some parts of the other chaos and creating the other chaos, and you'll find this chaos is completely different from the first chaos. Such a process exists innumerably. You always go back to the chaotic fiction. For example, you can find many different cells in each part of your body. And you can build a bridge between one cell and the other cell. You don't have to have a shape of human being. You can be a whole city. But this idea does not come from the training. Having diseases sometimes makes a building more attractive. Nothing can be obvious even if a halftrained body moved ostentatiously. I don't want to dance like that.

NOTES BY ANZU FURUKAWA

The Cuckoo

I am going to put my estranged body in a place where it can be free from the trappings of consciousness.

Whenever the time comes for me to call the dance in, a bird comes with a white cloth like the famous birthbird. But unlike the famous birthbird, it is not a stork, but a cuckoo.

Some five years ago in Goshogawara, a town in Tōhoku, I sprang from bed upon hearing the unique call of the cuckoo at dawn.

Before that I had seen a towering cedar tree at the dawn of day deep in the heart of the mountains in Toyama. The shock upon seeing it was so forceful and intense that my entire field of vision was flooded by the woody tree; raising my eyes in fear I saw how it soared way up into the heavens gradually getting thinner.

The two sensations fused, that of the tree and that of the cuckoo, forming a sensual fugue that wavered among my senses. I was so confused that I almost had to loosen my bowels.

The cuckoo cannot choose its song nor the tree its material; only human beings believe that they can choose how to live and how to die.

It is due to this arrogance that we are forced to fall and come face-to-face with our prime nature.

If I am asked about the nature of this dance I am put in a quandary, holding my head between my hands, my arms wrapped around my legs, clutching at the nearest thing in sight: maybe a baby, a fish, a mailbox, a wok, or even a tin bucket. It could well be that I danced in this fashion before. I can't tell; I'm not really sure this is the right thing—in this way I have qualified myself to be a human waste. When I want something frightening, I will have to make it myself.

I have never thought how to dance; I am just like a small fish in an endless sea called dance. This small fish plays her main role in the dreams of her spectators, but not in her own life. In the fantasies of the audience she wants to be a dangerous passenger...

"I have never thought how to dance; I am just like a small fish in an endless sea called dance. This small fish plays her main role in the dreams of her spectators, but not in her own life...."

NOTES BY YŌKO ASHIKAWA

My Work with Hijikata

It hadn't been more than six months that I had been working in butoh. I remember being alone in a cafe with Hijikata. We were talking enthusiastically about butoh, but as I was practically a beginner, I didn't understand everything he was saying. However, I tried to follow as best as I could. I wasn't really listening with my ears, rather I would place my ears near the knee, for example.

I remember him talking about the people he was watching pass in the street. "Actually, all those people are just carrying a dead shape."

At the time, I wasn't able to understand his comments, and the unexplained words could not build up in my body. And yet, I'm still very strongly aware of all those terribly important things which he passed on to the young girl I had been.

Hijikata's most interesting period of work began around 1972, with the "Tōhoku Kabuki" series and the beginning of rehearsals for "Twenty-seven Evenings for a Season." He developed his choreography, telling us about Akita and the region.

I thought that we couldn't possibly understand, being so young, but we understood fairly well. We weren't very experienced, so it was as if he was drawing on a blank page. When he said "Roll on the ground," I rolled on the ground; when he said "Walk bow-legged," I did. And he created the dance this way, marveling at this "magic box" emptying its contents before his eyes.

Our work was so enjoyable at the time! Hijikata would tell us to stick out our tongues and we would stick out our tongues, and then giggle to see how ugly we looked. At New Year's, we stuffed ourselves with rice cakes, then laughed at our swollen bellies. That was how we came to create such interesting dance work.

NOTES BY EBISU TŌRI & MIN TANAKA

The Lay of the Land

Children have secrets
Adults know nothing of
In their mortal bodies
Is a wasteland
Where vine and thorn are entangled
Refusing trespassers
Into its secret domain
A child's paradise
A labyrinth of wonders
While rummaging through my secret haunt
In that childlike state of grace
I found myself
Detached from the others
Abandoning my body in silence.
What is the body a shelter from?
It cannot be deceived by masks
Seeking to exist in itself
Not waiting on anybody or anything
But immersing itself in the present
Living its life and dying its death
Burying myself in my mortal flesh
I have grasped the sense of my body's way

Without words
Transformed
Observant
Distant
It allows me to stand without support
And dance.   E. Tōri

I am dancing a single dance throughout my life. My dance is identical with the everlasting revolution. I recovered my language through dancing, and saw politics through dancing. I will live up to ethics through dancing, and perceive the map of history through dancing. I gained the courage to stand against power through dancing. I am re-scrutinizing the "instinct" through dancing. I want to know God through dancing. I want to encounter matter through dancing. Anna Halperin, mother of American avant-garde, once said that dance is a way of life. I intend to be an authentic and legitimate child of dance initiated in ancient time. A dancer, in essence, is an anonymous lightning, a medium of the place. This is how I want to be. The endless performance/dance. An attempt to verify dance from the minimal to the maximal by rendering my body as an example. Or an attempt to discover and initiate dance in all places.   M. Tanaka

NOTES BY M. ISHII & N. NAKAJIMA

We have been meeting everyday with our body which has come from our mother's womb. It's ours, whether we are satisfied or not.

The hands have recognized how to touch, the legs have known how to walk.

Yet we find the body has been left.

Who let it become abandoned?

Only essence can make dance meaningful. The dancer has to find his own way to become identical with his own forms. Controlling and stopping ego and emotions is a new start towards his own process of organic growth.

—M. Ishii

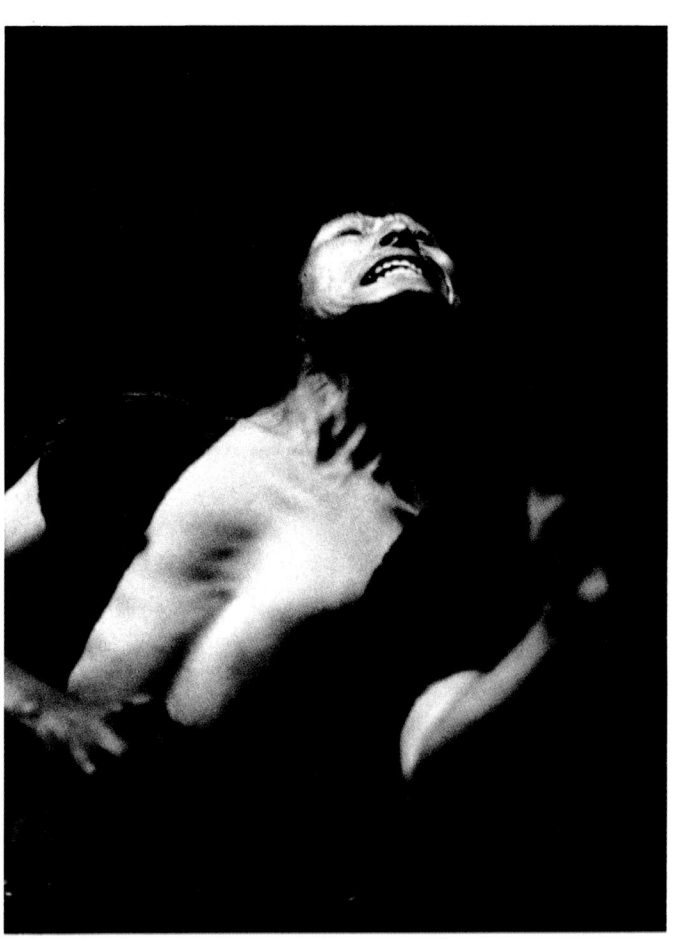

Sleep....
within the bosom of this shallow and yet deep sleep.
What does this sleeper dream of?
Sleeper lying down, dream wakes up.

Finally, just as smiles invite other smiles,
that huge smile spread in a ring.

Fragmented life regains itself,
strings towards everlasting darkness.

"Sleep & Reincarnation—from Empty Land"
by N. Nakajima

PHOTOGRAPHERS

Abe, Jun	Pages 116(Above), 118(Below), 120-121	Kazama, Hideo	Pages 117, 119			188(Below), 189(Below), 190(Below)
Birmingham, Lucy	Page 198(Below)	Masson-Sekine, Nourit	Pages 30, 31, 34, 36, 38-39, 41-43, 45-55, 58-59, 88-91, 92(Below), 93-95, 102-103, 104(Below), 105(Below), 106-107, 119, 124, 125(Above), 126, 132-137, 139, 140(Right/Above and Below), 141-142, 152, 153(Above/Right), 153(Below), 158, 163(Above), 165, 167, 168(Above), 170(Above), 175-179, 182(Below), 183, 188(Above), 190(Above), 191(Below), 192, 195(Below), 197, 198(Above), 199-201	Nojiri, Osamu	Pages 108, 111(Both), 112
Daidō, Kōsei	Page 14			Ogawa, Takayuki	Pages 149-151
Delahaye, Guy	Page 115(Below)			Okada, Masato	Pages 159-162, 163(Below)
Fuji Kōki	Page 168(Below/Left)			Onozuka, Makoto	Pages 13, 69-75, 82, 84, 185(Below), 189(Below/Second from the right)
Fujisaki, Tadashi	Pages 21, 24, 65, 147(Above), 148, 184, 188(Below/Second from the left)			Sakamoto, Masafumi	Pages 113, 114, 115(Above)
Hanaga, Mitsutoshi	Pages 8, 9, 10(Left/Above and Below), 11, 12, 16, 26, 35, 63-68, 83, 85-87, 98, 101, 104(Above), 105(Above), 122, 123(Both), 127-131, 147(Below), 153(Above/Left), 154-157, 169, 185(Above), 191(Above/Left), 196			Sawatari, Hajime	Page 191(Above/Right)
				Sugaya, Tesshin	Page 166(Below)
				Treatt, Nicolas	Page 166(Above)
				Tsukamoto, Hiroaki	Pages 33, 37, 58 59(Below/Right)
Hasegawa, Roku	Page 63(Above/Left)			Wallis, Robert	Page 15
Hashisaka, Toshi	Page 193(Above)	Moriya, Kaname	Pages 116(Below), 118(Above), 164	Yamaji, Kiyomi	Pages 109-110
Horiuchi, Nobushige	Page 168(Below/Right)			Yamada, Michihiro	Page 129(Below)
		Murata, Toshiei	Page 195(Above)	Yamazaki, Hiroto	Page 125(Below)
Hosoe, Eikō	Pages 19(Below), 25, 28-29, 31, 40, 61, 75-81, 186-187	Nakatani, Tadao	Pages 18, 19(Above), 63(Above/Right and Below), 64,	Yamazaki, Izumi	Pages 138, 170(Below)

PHOTO CREDITS

- P.8 Mitsutoshi Hanaga, "La Argentina," 1977.
- P.9 Mitsutoshi Hanaga, "Rebellion of the Body," 1968.
- P.10 *Left (Above):* Mitsutoshi Hanaga, hippies in the street of Tokyo, Late 60's.
  Left (Below): Mitsutoshi Hanaga, Street event by the Zero Dimension group, Late 60's.
  Right: Courtesy of Kyōdō Photo. Demonstration in front of the Diet building against the renewal of the U.S. Japan Mutual Treaty in 1960.
- P.11 Mitsutoshi Hanaga, Art performance by the Zero Dimension group, 1968.
- P.12 Mitsutoshi Hanaga, Jūro Kara and Reisen Lee of Jōkyō Gekijō.
- P.13 *Above:* Makoto Onozuka, Tatsumi Hijikata training at Asbesto-kan, Early 70's.
  Below: Event by Tenjō Sajiki.
- P.14 Kōsei Daidō, Shūji Terayama, 1968.
- P.15 *Above:* Robert Wallis, Fertility festival in Spring.
  Below: Courtesy of Shufunotomo, Hadaka Matsuri (Naked Festival).
- P.16 Courtesy of Mitsutoshi Hanaga, Baku Ishii.
- P.17 *Above:* Courtesy of Kazuo Ōno, Ōno and Hijikata during rehearsal, Late 50's.
  Below: Mitsutoshi Hanaga, Mitsutaka Ishii with K. Ōno and T. Hijikata in "Butoh Genet," 1967.
- P.18 Tadao Nakatani, Courtesy of Tomiko Takai, T.T. in "Emotion in Metaphysics," 1967.
- P.19 *Above:* Tadao Nakatani, Courtesy of Tomiko Takai, "Emotion in Metaphysics,"
(Left) T. Takai (Right) K. Ōno and T. Hijikata, 1967.
  Below: Eikō Hosoe, Yoshito Ōno in "Rose-colored Dance," 1965.
- P.21 Tadashi Fujisaki, Kazuo Ōno in his studio, 1970's.
- P.22 *Above:* Courtesy of Kazuo Ōno, A lesson of modern dance by Kazuo Ōno, Early 50's.
  Below: Courtesy of Kazuo Ōno, "Il pleut sur la ville comme il pleure dans mon cœur." Verlaine.
- P.23 Courtesy of Kazuo Ōno, Modern dance, 1949.
- P.24 Tadashi Fujisaki, Kazuo Ōno and Yoshito Ōno in "The Room," Late 50's.
- P.25 Eikō Hosoe, Tatsumi Hijikata and Kazuo Ōno in "Rose-colored Dance," 1965.
- P.26 Mitsutoshi Hanaga, "The Portrait of Mr.

P.27 Photo series from Chiaki Nagano Movies, 1969–73.
P.28–29 Eikō Hosoe, "La Argentina," 1977.
P.30 Nourit M.S., "La Argentina," 1985.
P.31 Eikō Hosoe, "La Argentina," 1977.
P.32 Nourit M.S., "La Argentina," 1984–85.
P.33 Hiroaki Tsukamoto, "La Argentina," 1985.
P.34 Nourit M.S., "My Mother," 1986.
P.35 Mitsutoshi Hanaga, "La Argentina," 1977.
P.36 Nourit M.S., "La Argentina," 1985.
P.37 Hiroaki Tsukamoto, "La Argentina."
P.38 Nourit M.S., "My Mother–Ozen," 1986.
P.39 Nourit M.S., "My Mother–Ozen," 1986.
P.40 Eikō Hosoe, "My Mother," 1981.
P.41 Nourit M.S., "My Mother–Ozen," 1986.
P.42 Nourit M.S., "My Mother," 1986.
P.43 Nourit M.S., "Dead Sea," Collage by Nourit M.S., 1985.
P.44 Courtesy of Kazuo Ōno, Ōno's mother and family picture.
P.45 Nourit M.S., "Dead Sea," 1985.
P.46 *Above:* Nourit M.S., Yoshito Ōno in "Dead Sea," 1985.
Below: Nourit M.S., "Dead Sea," 1985.
P.47 Nourit M.S., "Dead Sea," 1985.
P.48 Nourit M.S., Yoshito Ōno in "Dead Sea," 1986.
P.49 *Above:* Nourit M.S., Yoshito Ōno in "Water Lilies," 1987.
Below: Nourit M.S., Yoshito Ōno in "Dead Sea," 1986.
P.50 Nourit M.S., "Dead Sea," 1986.
P.51–53 Nourit M.S., "Dead Sea," 1985.
P.54 Nourit M.S., "Water Lilies," 1987.
P.55 Nourit M.S., A lesson in K. Ōno's studio, 1982.
P.58 *Below (Left):* Hiroaki Tsukamoto, Preparing for "La Argentina," 1977.
P.58–59 Nourit M.S., Hijikata and Ōno in rehearsal of "Dead Sea," 1985.
P.59 *Below (Right):* Hiroaki Tsukamoto
P.61 Eikō Hosoe, Portrait of Tatsumi Hijikata, 1968.
P.62 Courtesy of Asbesto-kan.
P.63 *Above (Left):* Roku Hasegawa "Rebellion of the Body," 1968.
P.63–64 Tadao Nakatami, "Rebellion of the Body," 1968.
P.65 Tadashi Fujisaki, early 70's.
P.66–68 Mitsutoshi Hanaga, "Rebellion of the Body," 1968.
P.69–71 Makoto Onozuka, "Shizukana Ie," 1973.
P.72 *Above:* Makoto Onozuka, "Shizukana Ie," 1973.
Below: Makoto Onozuka, "The Story of Small Pox," 1972.
P.73 Makoto Onozuka, "Shizukana Ie," 1973.
P.74–75 Makoto Onozuka, "Gibasan," 1972.
P.75–81 Eikō Hosoe, "Kamaitachi," 1967.
P.82 Makoto Onozuka, "Shizukana Ie," 1973.
P.83 Mitsutoshi Hanaga, "Rebellion of the Body," 1968.
P.84 Makoto Onozuka, The Story of Small Pox," Kōichi Tamano in the center, 1972.
P.85–87 Mitsutoshi Hanaga, Yōko Ashikawa in Kyōto University event, 1968.
P.88–89 Nourit M.S., "Tōhoku Kabuki" at Asbesto-kan, 1985.
P.90 Nourit M.S., Yōko Ashikawa in "Breast of Japan" at Plan B, 1983.
P.91 *Left:* Nourit M.S., Yōko Ashikawa in "Tōhoku Kakubi" at Asbesto-kan, 1985.
Right: Nourit M.S., Yōko Ashikawa in "Hook Off 88" at Plan B, 1983.
P.92 *Above:* Courtesy of T. Hijikata and Eikō Hosoe, From the catalogue for Hosoe's movie "The Navel and the Bomb," 1960's.
Below: Nourit M.S., Maijuku Group in Butoh festival, Dance choreographed by Tatsumi Hijikata, 1985.
P.93–95 Nourit M.S., Yōko Ashikawa in "Hook Off 88" at Plan B, 1983.
P.98 Mitsutoshi Hanaga, Dairakuda-kan's original members.
P.101 Mitsutoshi Hanaga, Event in 1977, Akaji Maro stands second from the right.
P.102 *Above:* Nourit M.S., Akaji Maro, 1982.
Below: Nourit M.S., Dairakuda-kan at Butoh Festival, 1987.
P.103 Nourit M.S., "The Book of Five Rings" by Dairakuda-kan, 1985.
P.104 *Above:* Mitsutoshi Hanaga, Dairakuda-kan.
Below: Nourit M.S., "The Book of Five Rings" by Dairakuda-kan, 1985.
P.105 *Above:* Mitsutoshi Hanaga, Dairakuda-kan.
Below: Nourit M.S., Dairakuda-kan at Butoh Festival, 1987.
P.106 Nourit M.S., Dairakuda-kan's member after performance in their theater, 1983.
P.107 Nourit M.S., Akaji Maro at Butoh Festival, 1985.
P.108 Osamu Nojiri, Ushio Amagatsu in "Kinkan Shōnen," 1978.
P.109 Kiyomi Yamaji, "Jomon."
P.110 *Above:* Kiyomi Yamaji, "Jomon," 1982.
Below: Kiyomi Yamaji, "Jomon," 1982.
P.111 *Above:* Osamu Nojiri, "Kinkan Shōnen."
Below: Osamu Nojiri, "Kinkan Shōnen."
P.112 Osamu Osamu Nojiri, "Kinkan Shōnen" at Nancy Festival, 1980.
P.113 Masafumi Sakamoto, U. Amagatsu in "Unetsu."
P.114 Masafumi Sakamoto, "Unetsu."
P.115 *Above:* Masafumi Sakamoto, U. Amagatsu in "Unetsu," 1986.
Below: Guy Delahaye, "Unetsu," 1986.
P.116 *Above:* June Abe, "Gourmet" series in Taiwan.
Below: Kaname Moriya, "Encounter with the Caterpillar" from "Alice" series in Taiwan, 1986.
P.117 *Above:* Hideo Kazama, Sanae Hiruta.
Below: Hideo Kazama, "The Last Supper" at Dead Sea, 1985.
P.118 *Above:* Kaname Moriya, "Eve in the Future" in Taiwan, 1986.
Below: Jun Abe, "Hibari to Nejaka" (Skylark and Lying Buddha) in Melbourne, 1987.
P.119 Hideo Kazama, Isamu Ōsuka.
P.120–121 Jun Abe, "Hyperpitvitarism Olympic" in a Christian cemetery in the Philippines, 1983.
P.122 Mitsutoshi Hanaga, "Liars Banquet," Anzu Furukawa in the center.
P.123 *Above:* Mitsutoshi Hanaga.
Below: Mitsutoshi Hanaga, Tamura and Furukawa in "Toyotama Story," 1980.
P.124 Nourit M.S., Tetsuro Tamura, 1985.
P.125 *Above:* Nourit M.S., Butoh Festival.
Below: Hiroto Yamazaki, "Le Prince des Sots," 1982.
P.126 Nourit M.S., A member of Dance Love Machine in rehearsal of Butoh Festival performance, 1985.
P.127 Mitsutoshi Hanaga, Ariadone (Carlotta Ikeda sitting in the middle).
P.128 Mitsutoshi Hanaga, Ariadone.
P.129 *Above:* Mitsutoshi Hanaga, Ariadone.
Below: Michihiro Yamada, Ariadone "Zarathustra."
P.130 Mitsutoshi Hanaga, Sebi.
P.131 Mitsutoshi Hanaga, Ariadone.
P.132–133 Nourit M.S., Natsu Nakajima in "The Garden," 1982.
P.134 Nourit M.S., Natsu Nakajima and Lili Maezawa, 1984.
P.135 *Above:* Nourit M.S., Natsu Nakajima in "The Garden," 1984.
Below: Nourit M.s., Lili Maezawa, 1982.
P.136 Nourit M.S., Natsu Nakajima, 1982.
P.137 Nourit M.S., Natsu Nakajima in "Sleep and Reincarnation from Empty Land," 1987.
P.138 *Above:* Izumi Yamazaki, Suzurantō.
Below: Izumi Yamazaki, Hoppō Butoh-ha.
P.139 Nourit M.S., Two People for Three Nights at Plan B, 1982.
P.140 *Left (Above and Below):* Courtesy of Gorō Namerikawa, Gorō Namerikawa, 1986–87.
Right (Above): Nourit M.S., Kōichi Tamano, 1987.
Right (Below): Nourit M.S., Tomiko Takai, 1986.
P.141 Nourit M.S., Mutsuko Tanaka of Tenkei-sha, 1986.
P.142 Nourit M.S., Yōko Ashikawa at Butoh Festival, 1987.
P.147 *Above:* Tadashi Fujisaki, Akira Kasai at Kōsei Nenkin Hall, 1967.
Below: Mitsutoshi Hanaga, Akira Kasai.
P.148 Tadashi Fujisaki, Akira Kasai.
P.149 Takayuki Ogawa, Events by Akira Kasai.
P.150–151 Takayuki Ogawa, Event by Akira Kasai.
P.152, 153 *Below:* Nourit M.S., Mitsutaka Ishii

and Betina Kleinhammes in "Mu dance," 1982.
P.153 *Above (Left):* Mitsutoshi Hanaga, Mitsutaka Ishii, 1960's.
Above (Right): Nourit M.S., Mitsutaka Ishii and Inoue the Jazz man.
P.154–157 Mitsutoshi Hanaga, Mitsutaka Ishii, late 60's and early 70's.
P.158 Nourit M.S., Min Tanaka at Plan B, 1983.
P.159 Masato Okada, At Yume-no-shima, 1977.
P.160 Masato Okada, Outdoor performance, 1980.
P.161 Masato Okada, "Renai Butoh-ha" choreographed by Tatsumi Hijikata, 1984.
P.162 Masato Okada, "The Shape of the Sky" at Plan B, 1984.
P.163 *Above:* Nourit M.S., At Plan B, 1983.
Below: Masato Okada, Min Tanaka.
P.164 *Above:* Kaname Moriya, Teru Goi at Plan B, 1983.
Below (Both): Kaname Moriya, Teru Goi.
P.165 Nourit M.S., Green Dance People at Terpsycore, 1987.
P.166 *Above:* Nicolas Treatt, Mitsuyo Uesugi, 1985.
Below: Tesshin Sugaya, Mitsuyo Uesugi, 1986.
P.167 *Above:* Nourit M.S., Minoru Hideshima, 1986.
Below: Nourit M.S., Setsuko Yamada, 1983.
P.168 *Above:* Nourit M.S., Butoh in the rice field for new year—Moritsuna Nakamura, 1986.
Below (Left): Kōki Fuji, Masaki Iwana in "Rain Moon."
Below (Right): Nobushige Horiuchi, Kunishi Kamirio in "Fool," 1977.
P.169 Mitsutoshi Hanaga, Nada Natsugiwa, 1983.
P.170 *Above:* Nourit M.S., Shirō Daimon, 1986.

Below: Izumi Yamazaki, Giriaku the traditional street performer.
P.175 Nourit M.S., Kazuo Ōno.
P.176 Nourit M.S., Kazuo Ōno in his studio.
P.175 *Above:* Nourit M.S., Moritsuna Nakamura, 1982.
Below (Left): Nourit M.S., Mitsuyo Uesugi, 1982.
Below (Right): Nourit M.S., Minoru Hideshima, 1982.
P.178–179 Nourit M.S., What is a lesson at Kazuo Ōno's studio, 1982–1986.
P.180 Courtesy of Kazuo Ōno, Drawing by Natsuyuki Nakanishi in which K. Ōno recognized "La Argentina."
P.181 *Above:* Courtesy of Kazuo Ōno, Antonia Mercé.
Below: Courtesy of Kazuo Ōno, Pamphlet and Poster by Eikō Hosoe for K. Ōno's performance, 1977.
P.182 *Above:* Courtesy of Kazuo Ōno, encounter with Antonia Merce bust in Spain.
Below: Nourit M.S., Dead Sea, 1985.
P.183 Nourit M.S., Kazuo Ōno and his wife in their kitchen, 1986.
P.184 Tadashi Fujisaki, Tatsumi Hijikata, Early 70's.
P.185 *Above:* Mitsutoshi Hanaga, Tatsumi HIjikata in his Asbesto-kan theater.
Below: Makoto Onozuka, Tatsumi Hijikata, Late 60's.
P.186–187 Eikō Hosoe, From "Kamaitachi," 1968.
P.188 *Above:* Nourit M.S., Butoh Festival, 1985.
P.188 *Below:* and P.189 *Below:* Courtesy of Tadao Nakatani, "Hijikata and the Japanese."
P.188 *Below (Second from the left):* Tadashi Fujisaki, Hijikata and the Japanese."
P.189 *Above:* Courtesy of Kazuo Ōno, Tatsumi Hijikata in the late 50's.
P.189 *Below (Second from the right):* Makoto

Onozuka, "Gibasan."
P.190 *Above:* Nourit M.S., Natsuyuki Nakanishi talking about Tatsumi Hijikata, 1984.
Below: Tadao Nakatani, Courtesy of Tomiko Takai, N. Nakanishi's body-painting on Hijikata's back, 1960's.
P.191 *Above (Left):* Mitsutoshi Hanaga, Akaji Maro in costume created by N. Nakanishi, 1970's.
Above (Right): Hajime Sawatari, Exhibition of N. Nakanishi's work, 1963.
Below: Nourit M.S., Lecture by Eikō Hosoe about the 60's and Hijikata at Asbesto-kan, 1986.
P.192 Nourit M.S., Exhibition of photographs "Homage to Hijikata" at Parco, Performance by Kazuo Ōno, 1987.
P.193 *Above:* Toshi Hashisaka, Kazuko Shiraishi, 1972.
Below: Poster for K. Shiraishi poetry dedicated to Kazuo Ōno.
P.194 From "Mementoes" of the late Yoshiyuki Takada, a member of Sankai-juku.
P.195 *Above:* Toshiei Murata, Isamu Ōsuka.
Below: Nourit M.S., Byakko-sha and fans after Butoh Festival performance, 1985.
P.196 Mitsutoshi Hanaga, Ushio Amagatsu.
P.197 Nourit M.S., Dairakuda-kan at Butoh Festival, 1987.
P.198 Nourit M.S., Dance Love Machine in rehearsal, A. Furukawa in the center, 1985.
P.199 Nourit M.S., Yōko Ashikawa at Butoh Festival, 1987.
P.200 *Above:* Nourit M.S., Ebisu Tōri.
Below: Lucy Birmingham, Min Tanaka.
P.201 *Above:* Nourit M.S.
Below: Nourit M.S., Exhibition of photographs "Homage to Hijikata" at Parco, Performance by N. Nakajima, 1987.

LIST OF NAMES

Akiyama 12
Amagatsu, Ushio 100, 101, 108, 114, 196
Andō, Mitsuko 62
Argentina, La 23, 26, 31, 34, 180, 182
Ashikawa, Yōko 84, 86, 88, 94, 97, 139, 142, 144, 173, 199

Bausch, Pina 16
Betsuyaku, Minoru 15
Blake, William 42
Brecht 13

Callas, Maria 31, 34
Cage, John 13
Chopin 44
Cunningham, Merce 16

Daimon, Shirō 170
Dazai, Osamu 11
Dalcroze 16

Eguchi, Takaya 24, 34, 62
Eiko and Koma 171

Falla 181
Fukuhara, Tetsurō 167
Furukawa, Anzu 122, 200

Genet, Jean 24, 64
Giriaku 170
Goi, Teru 164
Grotowski, Jerzy 22
Gunji, Masakatsu 15

Hagiwara, Sakutarō 184
Halley 183
Harada, Nobuo 167
Hemingway 24
Hijikata, Tatsumi 13, 14, 15, 16, 17, 19, 24–26, 60–96, 100, 108, 132, 138, 140, 147, 152, 167, 173, 176, 185, 188, 190, 192, 199
Hiruta, Sanae 116, 117
Horiuchi, K. 62
Hosoe, Eikō 92, 96, 97, 172, 191

Ikeda, Carlotta 127, 144, 145
Ikemiya, Nobuo 24
Ishii, Baku 16
Ishii, Mitsutaka 17, 19, 26, 84, 152, 172, 201
Iwana, Masaki 167, 168

Kamba, Michiko 10
Kamirio, Kunishi 165, 168
Kara, Jūrō 12, 13, 14, 15, 170
Kasai, Akira 26, 84, 147, 149, 150, 165, 167
Kawabata, Yasunari 11
Kimura, Tsunehisa 144
Kleinhammes, Bettina 52
Kobayashi, Saga 84
Kreutzberg, Harald 24, 34

Lautreamont 64
Lee, Rei Sen 12, 173

Maezawa, Lili 132, 135
Maro, Akaji 100, 101, 107, 197
Marin, Maguy 171
Matsudaira 12
Matsumura, Kazuko 62
Mercé, Antonia 26, 34
Mimura, Momoko 84
Mishima, Yukio 11, 62, 64
Monden, Yoshio 23, 180
Monet 183
Morita, Kenichi 40
Murobushi, Kō 101, 127

Nagamatsu 12
Nagano, Chiaki 26
Nakajima, Natsu 132, 135, 145, 173, 201
Nakamura, Moritsuna 167, 168
Nakanishi, Natsuyuki 26, 180, 190
Namerikawa, Gorō 140
Natsugiwa, Nada 169

Ōno, Kazuo 15, 17, 19–55, 62, 64, 84, 92, 132, 147, 152, 165, 193
Ōno, Yoshito 17, 19, 24, 45, 64, 84
Ōsuka, Isamu 101, 116, 119, 195

Ōta, Shōgo 170

Picasso 190

Sade 64
Satō, Makoto 13, 14, 15
Shimada 101
Shiraishi, Kazuko 192
Shiraishi, Poppo 171
Sonoda 12
Steiner, Rudolph 147
Suzuki, Shinichi 12
Suzuki, Tadashi 13, 14

Takada, Yoshiyuki 194
Takai, Tomiko 19, 26, 140
Takemitsu, Tōru 12
Takeuchi, Yasuko 26
Tamano, Kōichi 84, 140, 145
Tamura, Tetsurō 100, 101, 122
Tanaka, Min 92, 158, 161, 162, 173, 198
Tanaka, Mutsuko 141
Tanizaki, Junichirō 11
Terayama, Shūji 13, 14, 170
Tōri, Ebisu 101, 198

Uesugi, Mitsuyo 165
Uno, Man 140

Verlaine 22

Wigman, Mary 24, 62

Yamada, Bishop 100, 101, 138
Yamada, Kōsaku 16
Yamada, Setsuko 165
Yamaguchi 12
Yanagita, Kunio 11
Yaz-Kaz 108
Yokoo, Tadanori 14, 96
Yoshikawa, Yōichiro 108
Yoshimoto, Daisuku 170
Yotsuya, Simon 173
Yuki, Yūko 100, 101, 138

Glossary

Akutai Matsuri
A festival, or ritual in a festival, in which abusive language is used by villagers against a priest and against each other.

Ankoku Buyō
Dance (Buyō) of Darkness (Ankoku). A term originated by Tatsumi Hijikata to distinguish his new dance from the others. He later used the term *butoh* instead of *buyō*. (see "Butoh")

Biwa
A pear-shaped, plucked lute, usually with 4 or 5 strings. Brought from China in the late 7th century with many other instruments of court music. Used by both nobility and blind itinerant storytellers.

Bugaku
Court dances of slow and expansive movements with religious significance and accompanied by *gagaku*, the court music. Both of these artistic forms were introduced from China and Korea about the late 7th century. Due to their popularity at the Heian court (794–1185), many Japanese composers followed the Chinese example and wrote pieces in this style. Until the modern era these pieces were not known to the general public, as they were played only in the presence of the nobility.

Butoh
During the Meiji period it designated salon dances. This word had since become obsolete but has come into usage again recently, although its present meaning differs somewhat from the original. The word *butoh* is composed of the two ideographs 舞 *bu* (dance) and 踏 *toh* (step). It is a somewhat more concrete image of dance than the term *Buyō*.

Buyō
Dance. This word is written with two ideographs (舞踊) both meaning dance.

Dalcroze, Emile (1865–1950)
Swiss musician and pedagogue whose theories on movement and education had an enormous impact on the world of dance.

Eurythmics
The art of performing various bodily movements in rhythm, usually to musical accompaniment. A system devised by Rudolf Steiner.

Geta
A high wooden clog fastened to the foot by a thong between the first and second toes.

Grotowski, Jerzy (1933–)
Polish contemporary theater director, who runs a Theater Laboratory in Wroclaw. He is famous for his research on drama and on the actor's work.

Hangi Daitō-kan
"The mirror of the sacrifice in fire." This phrase was created by Yukio Mishima to describe the dance of Hijikata.

Hokkaidō
The northernmost of Japan's four main islands.

Kabuki
A form of Japanese drama dating from the 17th century. It is based on popular themes with male and female roles now performed exclusively by men, highly stylized with strong elements of dance, song and mime. Originally it consisted of risque dances performed by women, but due to a ban imposed by the then authorities the female roles were taken by young boys. There were several scandals including off-stage sexual activities with these young boys, and as a result they, too, were banned from performing. Finally they were replaced by mature actors. Famous dramatists such as Chikamatsu, Namboku, Mokuami and actors such as Danjurō and Tojurō, all contributed to developing this theatrical form, creating one of the most spectacular, colorful and dramatic stage presentations in the world.

Kagura
Folkloric or festive dances performed by villagers or townspeople during Shintō ceremonies. These dances go back many centuries.

Koto
Lute with 13 strings, placed horizontally on the floor when played.

Kreutzberg, Harald (1902–1968)
German dancer and choreographer. One of the most representative dancers of the German expressionist dance school.

Mai
Dance. This ideograph (舞) gives the impression of a slower, more horizontal dance than *Odori*; *Mai*

Meiji
denotes mainly the kind of dance performed in the *Nō* theater.

Meiji
Meiji period (1868–1912). The Meiji Restoration marked the end of the shogunate and the ancient feudal system. It also saw the opening of Japan after some 200 years of isolation from the outside world. Western influences began to filter into all fields of life, politics, science and the arts.

Modoki
In various Japanese folk and classic performing arts, a clown-like character who parodies and ridicules the main role (Sanbasō in the ceremonial *Nō* play "Okina" or "Hyottoko" in some *kagura*).

Namahage
A folk ritual in the Tōhoku area, usually taking place around mid-January. Young villagers, wearing fearsome masks and straw coats, enter houses shouting, roaring and frightening children and brides.

Nihon Buyō
A Japanese dance form originally created for use in *kabuki* but which subsequently has become an autonomous dance form influenced by various traditional dance forms.

Nō
A classic form of Japanese drama with choral music and dancing, using set themes, simple symbolic scenery, elaborately masked and costumed performers and stylized acting. Founded at the end of the 14th century by Kan'ami and his son Zeami, *Nō* incorporates elements of the most archaic forms of Japanese theater such as the *dengaku* (peasant dances) and *sarugaku* (buffoonery). The themes are extremely rudimentary and cover subjects such as filial piety, love, jealousy, revenge and the samurai spirit.

Odori
Also signifies dance, but connotes a quicker paced and more lively dance form than *mai*. *Odori* denotes mainly the kind of dance performed in *kabuki* theater.

Sakhalin
An island of the USSR in the northern Pacific Ocean. Japanese colonists lived in the southern part of Sakhalin in the late 18th century, and Russians in the north. The two powers ruled jointly until 1875. In 1945 the USSR was ceded the southern part of the island.

Shakuhachi
End-blown notched flute made of bamboo, with four finger holes and one thumb hole. Originally came from China around the early 8th century.

Shamisen
Japanese musical string instrument somewhat like a banjo but with three strings.

Shingeki
"New theater"; a movement established in the 1920's. It rejected the Japanese traditional theater and adopted Western models of dramatic and theatrical expression.

Stanislavski, Konstantin Sergeevich (1863–1938)
Russian actor and theater director, director of the Art Theater of Moscow. His systematic training method for actors is one of the most famous in the world.

Steiner, Rudolf (1861–1925)
Austrian social philosopher; founder of the spiritualistic doctrine known as anthropology.

Tatami
A floor mat of woven rice straw used traditionally in Japanese homes.

Tōhoku
The northern region of Honshu (the main island of the Japanese archipelago).

Wigman, Mary (1886–1973)
German dancer, choreographer and teacher; the most famous expressionist dancer.

Zengakuren
Student association active prior to the renewal of Japanese-American mutual security treaty in 1960 and during the events of the 60s.

Zōri
Japanese straw sandals, consisting of a flat sole attached to the foot by means of a straw thong between the first and second toes.